LIVING BY FAITH

God's miraculous hand in the life, times and journey of Gerry Gallimore

"Come and listen, all you who fear God; let me tell you what He has done for me."
– Psalm 66:16

Dedication

Dedicated to the honor and memory of those
who profoundly influenced and shaped my life
by their love, their time, their prayers, their
counsel and their godly example.

L. G. Coke
Sonia Gallimore
Rupert Gallimore
Olga Coke
Daphne Logan
Merle Brown
Roderick James
Errol Miller
William Edwards
Burchell Taylor
Clinton Webb
Jim Groen
Werner Burklin
Robert Levy
Cecil Parke
Bethel Baptist Church
Metropolitan Baptist Church
Plymouth Brethren Assemblies
Colleagues in Youth For Christ Int'l
(and many others too numerous to mention by name)

4

Table of Contents

6

At 31 years of age

Background

As I write this I am 82+ years of age. By God's grace and His keeping power I have passed the threescore years and 10 and am into the "by reason of strength" (Ps.90:10) period of life. So much – yes, so very much to thank God for! Mine has been a marvelous journey of rich faith adventures, rich ministry associations, and above all rich experiences with God…and for God!

I should have done this a long time ago. It was Rev. Cleve Grant (renowned Jamaican Church of God pastor of blessed memory) who first implored me over 40 years ago to put these God-stories in writing. Numerous others have encouraged me over the years. I thought when I retired from the pastorate in January 2006 that I would have ample time to write. Little did I guess how busy the Lord was going to keep me in the preaching of His Word, in counseling, in mentoring, and in giving leadership to various aspects of Christian ministry! To His name be praise and glory!

I am still busy and just as excited about preaching the Word and sharing the soul-saving good news of salvation by faith in the finished work of the Cross! The Lord willing, I will keep on doing this until He calls me home.

But now before my memory fades I invite you, in the words of the Psalmist, *"Come and listen, all you who fear God; and let me tell you what He has done for me"* (Psalm 66:16).

No doubt God has done even greater things for you. He is that kind of God – good, faithful and without partiality. I rejoice with you with loud "Amens." But this is <u>my</u> story for which I beg permission to share with you in honor of the Lord, to bring glory to His name…and to be an encouragement to you and to others.

So here goes.

My registered name is Gerald Osborne Gallimore, but better known as Gerry Gallimore. I was born in the parish of St. Ann in the island of Jamaica on August 29, 1938 to humble circumstances (that's for another writing). In the providence of God I was raised by my aunt and her husband, Lillian & Lifford Coke – both of whom were teachers at Bethany Elementary School, of which Lifford Coke was principal. Theirs was a godly home.

Lifford Coke remains for me one of the most godly men I have ever known. I grew up in his home so I knew him at close range. A man of unswerving Christian commitment issuing in a life of compelling character, integrity, compassion and service. His influence on my life was, and remains profound, despite the fact that he has been dead nearly 50 years! I hope, I pray and I live trusting the Lord that my life may influence someone in the way his life has influenced mine! While I recognize and am grateful for the many others who have contributed to the quality of my life, I realize now that in L.G. Coke God drew near and shaped my life by this man's words, by his influence, his love and care, and the high expectations he had of me. *Thank you once again Father, for my aunt and uncle-in-law. Whatever I have become or have achieved that is of any worth, I owe it to You through them.*

On a never to be forgotten day, September 23, 1953, I surrendered my heart to the Lord Jesus Christ in a Gospel service at Bethany Baptist Church, St. Ann, Jamaica under the preaching of Mr. Dudley Cammock and received Jesus Christ as my personal Savior and Lord. I was baptized 4 months later.

I began 'preaching' at age 17. I was president of my high school's Student Christian Movement and as such had to prepare devotionals for our weekly meetings. That is where it began.

In 1956 I moved from Bethany, St. Ann, to the city of Kingston in Jamaica and became a part of a dynamic young church – Bethel Baptist Church comprised of young people about my then age. Bethel Baptist Church was to play a major role in my spiritual development for the next 33 years. By age 20, I was Deacon, Church Secretary, Church Trustee, Sunday School teacher, Training Union leader, Youth Fellowship leader and lay preacher.

That same year 1956 I started attending Youth For Christ Saturday night rallies in Kingston. I soon became a part of the YFC planning team, speaking at the rallies, while also involved with Child Evangelism Fellowship; helping out at Barbican Baptist Church and sharing in prison ministry under the leadership of Rev. Dr. J.A. Leo-Rhynie of East Queen Street Baptist Church.

I became involved as well with a group of largely Brethren young people called Ambassadors For Christ that held open-air lunch-hour meetings in the parks in the capital city of Kingston (Jamaica).

In 1958 my cousin Olga Coke encouraged a number of us young people at Bethel Baptist Church to attend Keswick Convention in Mandeville, thereby introducing myself and several others to a ministry that was to play an important part in my life ever since. God used the guest speaker, Dr. Stephen Olford, at that Mandeville Keswick Convention in 1958, in a life changing way. Under his anointed ministry I, along with many others, encountered the Lord in a deep Holy Spirit experience that has marked my life ever since.

Alongside of all my other Christian activities and responsibilities, I became an itinerant evangelist doing Crusades all across Jamaica. I would leave my secular job at 4.00pm, grab a bite, drive to locations all across Jamaica, preach the Gospel, return home for some sleep, get to the job at 8:30am the following morning, to repeat it all over again a week at a time. We were sold out to the Lord and the Lord blessed, protected and energized us. Hallelujah!

Kingston Keswick Convention started in January 1961, meeting at Ardenne High School auditorium with Dr. Stephen Olford as the main speaker. It was another great week of ministry under the anointed preaching of Dr. Olford. On the Friday night of that week I heard and answered the call of God for full-time Christian ministry and publicly walked forward to surrender my life to that call. I continued working in secular employment and remained active in Christian service as I prayerfully waited for further direction from the Holy Spirit.

In July 1961, I met and fell in love with the beautiful Sonia Wright. In those days I worked at United Printers located on the outskirts of the city of Kingston. After work on Saturdays I would drive to the heart of the city for window shopping on King Street, the main commercial sector. There on this busiest street at the busiest hour on a Saturday, was a group of young people holding a Gospel meeting!

Although a committed Christian that kind of Christian witness seemed too fanatical to me, and so I was kind of disdainfully walking by when the most beautiful thing I had ever seen handed me a tract...and I was attracted. The following week I walked down King Street hoping that there would be an open-air gospel meeting by the same young people – and there was. This time I joined the group and shared in the meeting. At the end of the meeting against her much resistance I persuaded this young lady to let me give her a drive home (another interesting story ...) and, as they say, the rest is history. We were married on 23rd February 1963.

By 1968 I was doing well in in my business career. Sonia and I had a nice home in Drumblair, I drove a Mercedes-Benz, earned enough for my wife to be a stay-home mom with our two children – and I remained deeply involved at Bethel Baptist Church, in Youth For Christ, in crusade evangelism - among other things.

Every day in our devotions my wife Sonia would pray, "Lord, when is Gerry going to leave business to go into your work full-time?" And I would think, "foolish woman – doesn't she know a man has to provide for his family? And can't she see how involved I am in the work of the Lord?"

In that same year 1968 my boss at Mead Johnson (Jamaica) Limited, Mr. Hugh Rose, informed me of a significant promotion on the job and of the additional financial rewards that would be forthcoming. I went into the men's room to talk to the Lord in secret and to thank Him for this good news. But as I prayed I said to the Lord, "Lord, why am I not feeling elated? This is the best news a young man of my age could hear so why am I not feeling elated?" And the Lord said to me, "Are you sure this is what I want you to do?" I became troubled in my soul but would not share this with my wife Sonia since I knew exactly what she would say.

The commitment I made seven years earlier to full-time Christian service was brought forcibly to my mind. I kept all of this to myself.

In the midst of this spiritual crisis I received a
phone call from Rev. Werner Burklin, a German
YFC leader who had come to Jamaica to
organize a Youth For Christ International World
Conference and was wrapping up things to
return to Germany.

He invited me to lunch that day. As we sat
down at lunch he said to me, "Gerry, I have
invited you to lunch to tell you that the Lord
wants you in the ministry of Jamaica Youth For
Christ!" I was blown away. I had told no one of
all that was going on in my soul. I blurted out in
response to his statement, "But how could
anyone know?" Werner said to me, "Everyone
knows – I have spoken to four Christian leaders
before talking to you today and each one said to
me Gerry Gallimore is the person for this role." I
was flabbergasted.

At that time Jamaica Youth For Christ had
nothing but debts. I knew this because I was one
of the persons with a monthly pledge to help the
organization. Youth For Christ is a faith
organization with no salary commitments. Staff
members trust God for their financial support. I
needed time to think and pray this over. I had
no option then but to tell Sonia what was going
on. Her only response was, "so when are you
sending in your resignation?" Right about this
time as well Jamaica experienced a student

uprising which caused considerable damage and disruption to many businesses in the city of Kingston.

I wrestled for three months with this question about trusting God with our future; about resigning from the job and lifestyle which we enjoyed. During that time I consulted with several Christian leaders and with some family members as I prayed for the Lord's direction. I discovered that it was much easier to preach about trusting God than to step out in faith and trust God to provide!

It came to a head about 4.00am one morning when I awoke to spiritual warfare in my bedroom. One voice said to me don't do it – look how much you would be giving up; you have a great future in business with even more success in the future. The other voice – the voice of the Lord only promised me the cross. That battle went on for quite a while – and then I shouted out loud, "Okay Lord, you win. I will do it." With that the sweet peace of God descended on my spirit. I woke Sonia up and together we fell on our knees and committed it to the Lord.

My boss at Mead Johnson (Ja) Ltd, Hugh Rose, and I had a great relationship. I knew that turning in my resignation was not going to be

easy (but that is another story for another time).
December 31, 1968 was my last day at Mead
Johnson. Mr. Rose called the entire staff together
for what turned out to be an emotional farewell.
I had had a wonderful time of service at Mead
Johnson and my warm relationship with Mr.
Hugh Rose has remained to this day 50 years
later!

Beginnings

"Come and listen, all you who fear God; let me tell you what He has done for me." – Psalm 66:16

The Psalmist was not quiet about his faith nor about rejoicing in and publicizing the things that the Lord had done for him. We need to follow his example. Hear him in Psalm 34:

"I will bless the Lord at all times His praise shall continually be in my mouth. My soul shall make her boast in the Lord; the humble shall hear thereof and be glad. O magnify the Lord with me and let us exalt His name together."

In Psalm 100:4:
"Enter His Gates with thanksgiving and come into His courts with praise."

And in the opening verses of Psalm 66:
"Make a joyful shout to God, all the earth! Sing out the honor of His name; make His praise glorious."

And again in verse 8:
"O bless our God you peoples and make the voice of His praise to be heard."

So he issues this invitation, *"Come and listen, all you who fear God; let me tell you what He has done for me"* or as the NKJV puts it *"Come and hear all you who fear God and I will declare what He has done for my soul."* There is something on his heart bubbling over that he can't keep quiet about. He has to tell somebody. It is too much to keep to himself--so he issues an invitation for folks to gather around him, "Come" he says, "Come and listen, I have got something to tell you."

I share the Psalmist's conviction.

Some things we simply can't keep quiet about. Like the Psalmist we must share them. They are too good to keep only to ourselves. I am emboldened by the Psalmist's example to share the following stories of the Lord's miraculous provision for us as we have lived by faith, trusting Him to provide for our needs as we serve Him by faith.

Notice firstly, THE PERSONAL NATURE OF WHAT THE PSALMIST WOULD DECLARE. He wants to talk about what God has done for <u>him personally</u>! He is not now going to revel in the mighty acts of God in history. He is not going to call attention to God's majestic display of His power in creation—he is not even going to talk about what God has done for His church or

His people in general, BUT WHAT GOD HAS
DONE FOR HIM! He has a personal testimony.
God has been good to him and the Psalmist
wants to tell it out. What about us…what about
you, my brothers and sisters? Has God been
good to you? Do we have anything to
declare...to talk about...to invite folks to come
and listen to??

Notice in the second place, TO WHOM THE
PSALMIST FEELS FREE TO SHARE HIS
TESTIMONY. It is to "YOU WHO FEAR GOD."
Some things can only be shared with people of
like faith. They alone can understand—they
alone will listen with interest. Not everybody
will understand. Some will think you have lost a
screw. Not everybody out there will be blessed
and will join you in praising God. It is only those
of like faith, who themselves fear God. And so
believing that you will not think that I have lost
a screw, or that I am crazy, I would like to join
the Psalmist in saying "Come and listen and LET
ME TELL YOU ABOUT WHAT GOD HAS
DONE FOR ME!

I started working at Jamaica Youth For Christ as
National Director on January 2, 1969, at a small
rented office at 2 Haining Road, in Cross Roads,
Kingston, Jamaica. A committed Christian
young lady by the name of Camille Hart served
as secretary. YFC ministry at that time

consisted of Saturday night YFC Rallies in
Kingston, Mandeville and Montego Bay.

Within a few weeks Sonia and I had used up our
financial reserves and faced the first challenge to
living by faith. I had a wife, small children to
care for, but we were now out of money and out
of food! Sonia and I prayed about the situation
and I went off to the YFCI office that morning –
a Monday morning – with understandably an
urgent prayer and great concern on my heart.
At around 10.00am the mailman arrived. The
first letter I opened was one from the President
of Youth For Christ International, Dr. Sam
Wolgemuth, which simply said, "Dear Gerry, I
want you to know that we prayed for you this
morning. Whatever challenges you may be
facing remember that God is faithful and He will
see you through…" I immediately felt rebuked
in my spirit as this letter sparked assurance in
my heart that God would come through for us. I
immediately picked up the phone and
called my dear friend and brother in Christ,
Roderick James, and shared with him our
situation and then read him Dr.Wolgemuth's
letter, rejoicing at the timing of it and felt it was
a word from the Lord to my heart. He prayed
with me and I hung up the phone. Immediately
I hung up the phone, it rang and the stern voice
of a Christian lady rebuked me for being so long
on the phone as she had called several times.

Then she said, "stop by my house on your way home from office this afternoon." I hung up with distress in my spirit wondering what I was guilty of and what further reprimand I was in for from this stern believer.

I stopped by her house on my way home. She came out to me with two supermarket paper bags filled with groceries! I took them from her feeling greatly rebuked in my heart for the unkind thoughts I had carried all day, and at the same time my heart overflowing with gratitude to God. I was still holding the groceries with tears running down my face when she came back out with a crate of soft drinks (sodas). I thanked her profusely and drove home. Everything we needed by way of groceries was all there!

"Come and listen you that fear the Lord and let me tell you what the Lord has done for me."

That was just the beginning of our journey of living by faith and of how the Lord would again and again provide for our needs.

That same year 1969 our first child, Trudy, turned three in August. Age 3 is when we in Jamaica begin sending our children to prep school (kindergarten). The most famous prep school in Jamaica at that time was Vaz Prep

School; a private prep school founded and headed by Mrs. Hazel Vaz, a deeply committed Christian lady belonging to the Plymouth Brethren Assemblies in Kingston, Jamaica. Vaz Prep School was not only the coveted school for providing Christian education but also for achieving national distinction in all aspects of academic and cultural disciplines. Additionally, it was the place where our friends and associates sent their children. Sonia and I earnestly wanted Trudy to attend Vaz Prep School, but we had no way of affording the school fees. We committed this matter to the Lord and at the time of registration for the school year beginning August 1969, in a bold act of faith I went to see the principal, Mrs. Hazel Vaz.

When it was my turn, I went in to speak with Mrs. Vaz. I introduced myself, explained that my daughter was three years old and that we dearly wanted her to attend Vaz Prep School, but that we live by faith and had no idea how we could pay the school fees. At that point Mrs. Vaz said to me, "Mr. Gallimore, you do not know me personally but I know you for I have been in church every time you have spoken at Galilee Gospel Hall and the Lord has blessed me each time you have preached the Word. As long as I am principal here your daughter will attend Vaz Prep school at no cost and further I will extend the same privilege to each of your children!" You can imagine the hallelujah – the joy that overflowed my heart for God's amazing provision!! The school fees at that time were $200 per term (3 terms per year). Trudy, Oliver and Lisa (our three children) all attended Vaz Prep School for 8 years each without our ever paying school fees! Thanks be to God, and thanks be to His servant Mrs. Hazel Vaz!

I join with the Psalmist in shouting, *"Come you that fear the Lord and let me tell you what He has done for me."*

Building!

"I will bless the Lord at all times…
His praise shall continually be in my mouth."

Towards the end of 1969 the Lord did something
very special for us. The company where I
worked prior to answering God's call for
ministry, Mead Johnson (Ja.) Limited bought
property in Kingston to begin manufacture.
There was a small two bedroom cottage on the
property which was not going to be immediately
needed by the company. My former boss, Mr.
Hugh Rose very kindly offered us the use of that
cottage for our YFC office at no expense!
Needless to say, this was a tremendous
provision saving us the cost of monthly rental.
By that time young Barry Davidson (now Dr.
Barry Davidson of Family Life Ministries fame)
had joined our staff and so the extra space at this
new location was very valuable. This provision
of the Lord was marked with great joy as
another evidence of His hand of blessing on our
life of faith and on YFC's mission of reaching
young people with the saving message of the
Gospel.

"Come and listen you that fear the Lord and let me
tell you what He has done for me!"

The year was 1972. We were celebrating the 25th anniversary of Youth For Christ in Jamaica, which started back in 1947 by God's servant Mr. George Forbes. It was right at this time that Mr. Hugh Rose advised that regretfully the company would be needing the facility we were occupying and served notice that we would need to relocate. We went to the Lord in prayer asking for His provision once again, but with this added feature – we needed a place of our own. After 25 years of ministering to the youth of Jamaica, I felt like the time had come for YFC to have a place of its own from which to carry on ministry across the island. We laid this out before the Lord and asked for His direction and provision.

At home one morning while reading the daily newspaper, The Gleaner, my eyes fell on a 2"x 2-column ad by a firm of lawyers inviting bids on a house in the Cross Roads area (2 Acacia Avenue, Kingston 5). I finished reading the newspaper but for some reason I kept going back to that ad. I went to the office that morning and right after our staff devotions I shared with Barry Davidson and Lloyd Burnett (a young evangelist who was a part of our volunteer team) the ad in the newspaper and suggested we go to look at the property. It was a lot of about 100' x 100', overgrown with weeds with a house – but we loved the location for a possible YFC office in that it was in walking distance from the bus stop and near to the popular Tastee Patties production and retail center. The three of us got excited by its possibilities. Together we decided we would take a step of faith. Remembering what the Lord said to Moses and to Joshua that "Every place on which the sole of your foot treads shall be yours," we decided to walk by faith through the length and breadth of the property. Standing under a mango tree at the front step of the house the three of us locked arms together, bowed our heads in prayer and claimed it in the name of the Lord for the future office of Jamaica Youth For Christ! We hardly knew what to say to each other – it was a brand-new kind of experience for the three of us.

We drove back to the office in silence each one of us processing in our hearts what we had just done. Shortly after we got back to the office the mail came and the secretary brought a letter addressed to me personally.

I opened the letter and could hardly believe what I read. It was a letter from Mr. O. D. Sanguinetti, a beloved Christian businessman from the Plymouth Brethren community, and this is what it said, "My Dear Gerry, my wife and I have with delight watched the ministry of Youth For Christ grow under your leadership. The Lord has impressed our hearts that it is time for YFC to have a place of its own and so we enclose our check for $2000 to start you on a YFC headquarters building fund." You can imagine the impact this had on me – I could hardly believe my eyes. I shouted out to Barry and Lloyd and said to them, "you won't believe this – you won't believe this. You know what we just did a moment ago. Listen to this!" And I read them the letter. It was a hallelujah, Praise the Lord, tear-jerking moment.

"Come and listen you that fear the Lord and let me tell you what He has done for me!"

I immediately called up the chairman of our Jamaica YFC board, Mr. Peter Evelyn. Excitedly I said to him, "Bro. Peter, we have a major development in YFC, but I do not need the board to approve it, for the real chairman of the board has already sanctioned it!" And with that I told him about the newspaper ad, about what Barry, Lloyd and I had done, and I read him the letter from Bro. Sanguinetti. Peter joined in rejoicing over this miraculous provision of the Lord, and immediately said, "I will add $1500 to that!"

Needless to say I was anxious to put in a bid on behalf of Jamaica YFC, but I was totally inexperienced in that kind of transaction, so we started looking to the Lord to direct us.

Someone at that time suggested the name of a beloved servant of God, Mr. Karl Richards, the retired head of Victoria Mutual Building Society. I did not know the gentleman, but made an appointment to see him at his home. He received me graciously. With an overflowing heart I shared with him this miraculous development in Jamaica YFC, asking for his counsel and help. I could hardly believe my ears when the gentleman said to me, "Brother Gerry, you may not know, but I was one of the founding members of the first board of Jamaica YFC many years ago. In addition, the firm of lawyers in question are the lawyers for Victoria Mutual Building Society and so I know them very well." With that he picked up the phone, called the lawyers and inquired about the property for which they were asking bids. He then asked privileged information about the reserve figure below which they would not go. They told him. I then said to him, "So what offer do you recommend that I make?" He said, "I suggest that you go to their office by tomorrow and offer this reserve figure with a 10% deposit so they will know you are serious."

With great excitement in my heart I quickly called the board chairman of Jamaica YFC and other board members by phone and got their approval. Then I called up several of our prayer partners and asked them to pray. The following morning I dropped off at the lawyer's office my letter offering the reserve figure along with a check representing 10% of the offer.

Word spread quickly within the Christian community about this exciting development. Right in that period of time I was in Barbados doing an evangelistic mission at the Barbados campus of the University of the West Indies, when my wife Sonia called excitedly to tell me that a Christian gentleman in Jamaica hearing of what God was doing had offered to match up to $10,000 any amount raised towards getting a mortgage! Hallelujah! It blew me away. I had never before heard of or experienced something like this.

I went to Victoria Mutual Building Society to apply for the mortgage. They graciously afforded us a 20 year mortgage so we could complete the purchase. When I left VMBS office that day I stood on the step outside the office door lifted my hands to heaven praising God for what He had done. "Thank you Jesus! Thank you Lord – but 20 years is too long to be paid for this property!" God heard that prayer. We paid it off in three years!

"Come and listen you that fear the Lord and let me tell you what He has done for me!"

Yes…"*I will bless the Lord at all times…His praise shall continually be in my mouth."*

(As I write this 48 years later, this property still remains the Head Office of the island-wide ministry of Jamaica YFC. *To God be the glory!*)

Blessing

"My God shall supply all your need according to His riches in glory by Christ Jesus." Phil. 4:19

Finance to keep the ministry going is one of the challenges for every faith ministry. Jamaica Youth For Christ was/is no exception. As YFC ministry continued to make increasing impact across Jamaica a number of talented Christian young people were drawn to join staff. As the leader of the team it was my task to let them know that YFC was a faith ministry, that I could not guarantee their salary, but that we all looked to the Lord together and individually for the funding to cover the expenses of the ministry. In 1973 we had 8 members of staff serving at the national office. We met in my office on a Monday morning for weekly staff devotions. It was one of those times when I had to share with the staff of 8 that we had no money to meet the payroll that coming Wednesday. We needed $3500 and so I asked each of the eight of us to take turns asking the Lord to supply.

Wednesday came and there was no money.
It is an uncomfortable responsibility when as the 'boss' I must tell staff they would be getting no

paycheck and urged everyone to continue praying. The week ended and no funds. At around 9.00am the following Monday morning I was over by our Gospel Films department when a gentleman came through the door of the office. As he came through the door the Spirit said to me, "That's the man." I walked up to him, did not greet him with the usual "Good morning" instead I simply said to him, "Did you bring it?" He looked at me somewhat strangely and said, "I do not know." At that moment he took an envelope from his pocket and handed it to me. I opened the envelope and in it was a check for $1000! I lifted the envelope to heaven and said, "Thank you Father." Then I looked at the man and said to him, "Did you bring anything else?" He looked at me quite puzzled and said, "I don't understand." I said to him, "Come with me to my office." I did not offer him a seat. I said to him, "Sir, last week Monday morning the 8 of us on staff sat in this office and prayed to the Lord about our financial situation. We needed $3500 to pay staff last week Wednesday and so I asked each member of staff to ask the Lord to send us $3500. As you walked through the door this morning the Lord said to me, "That's the man." You gave me this envelope at $1000 so I ask you again did you bring anything else?"

The man looked at me like he had seen a ghost. He said out loud, "Jesus Christ" as he sat slowly

in a chair. He said to me, "you won't believe
this. I sold a piece of land in Mandeville (a city
in the middle of the island) for $25,000 and said
to my wife this morning, I believe the Lord
wants me to tithe this money. And with that he
took out his checkbook and wrote a check for
$2500. I lifted both checks to the Lord and with
a heart overflowing with praise and
thanksgiving gave the Lord thanks for his
marvelous provision. The man himself was
rejoicing with praise to the Lord sensing that he
was an instrument in the Lord's hand. I called
in the other seven members of staff and
reminded them about what we prayed for that
previous Monday. I told them what had just
happened and asked each one of them to lift the
two checks to the Lord in personal thanksgiving
for answering our prayer.

*"Come and listen you that fear the Lord and let me
tell you what He has done for me!"*
*"I will bless the Lord at all times…His praise shall
continually be in my mouth."*

*"My God shall supply all your need according to His
riches in glory by Christ Jesus."*

I will never forget that Wednesday evening in
the end of July in the year 1975 when Owen, one
of our young volunteers came by the Jamaica
YFC office and asked to see me. He said, "I

don't think you know that I work at the mortgage division of a bank in the city" – the bank which held the mortgage on our house. He informed me that the bank was reviewing delinquent accounts that morning and he was surprised to see my name among the delinquent accounts and that my name had been assigned to an aggressive collector, and so he was warning me to expect an unpleasant call soon. He then said to me, "Why did you allow your mortgage to fall so far in arrears?" With great embarrassment I had to tell him it fell in arrears because we had no money to pay it. He wanted to know what I was going to do? – what would I tell the collector? And warned me that the bank could repossess our house!

When Owen left the office I had a real problem with my Father. I paced the floor in my office saying, "Father, you called me to lead and mentor the young people who work with me in winning the unsaved. But how can I lead and mentor young people when they come in here to reprimand me about nonpayment of bills? Please Father, provide some money – please take me out of this predicament." The embarrassment of this shook me deeply - the reprimand of this youth – the delinquency in our mortgage payment, and the thought that the bank could repossess the house in which Sonia and I and our three children lived…was frightening to say the least.

I went home that night and shared with Sonia. In her usual manner she was confident that, "The Lord will come through for us." We prayed about it…Wednesday night, Thursday, Friday, Saturday, Sunday… but still no answer – no provision.

On the Monday morning while getting dressed for the office my phone rang. Mr. Souhail Karram, a Christian businessman who operated Elite Haberdashery store in downtown Kingston, and who at that time lived between Kingston Jamaica and Boca Raton, Florida; was on the phone. After a brief greeting he asked me, "Gerry, how are things?" I said, "Fine." We chatted briefly and the call was ended. My wife Sonia asked me about the call. I told her. She was not happy with my response to Mr. Karram. I said to her, "But sweetheart, I can't go spilling my guts to everybody who calls on the phone?" But the more I thought about it the more I wondered why Mr. Karram asked that question.

Shortly after I got to the office that morning the phone rang again and Mr. Karram was on the line. He asked the question again, "Gerry, tell me truthfully, how are things?" I demurred. He immediately said, "Come down to the office to see me."

I went down to his office at Elite Haberdashery on Princess Street. As I walked into his office he asked me for the third time, "How are things with you?" By then I sensed that the Lord was up to something. So I shared with him about the delinquency in our mortgage payments and about the embarrassment with Owen the previous Wednesday evening. He said to me, "Gerry last week Wednesday night the Lord woke me up in Boca Raton with a burden on my heart for you. I prayed for you but the burden would not go away until I got down on my knees by the side of my bed and prayed for you. _How much do you owe_?"

I made a very quick calculation and told him it was "about $1000" (the mortgage was just over $326 per month). With that he opened a filing folder on his desk and handed me an envelope with $1000 in cash in it!! He said to me, "The Lord told me to give you $1000." I was so overjoyed I didn't know how to thank him. All I wanted to do was to be able to call Sonia and tell her of the Lord's miraculous provision to pay up the back mortgage on our house.

I am stepping out of his office when he called me back and said to me, "Sit down – isn't there another need?" I thought about it quickly. Yes, there was another need. I told him our three children were due to start back at Vaz Prep School in a few days' time and we needed to get some supplies for them. He asked me, "How much do you need?" I did a very quick estimate for shoes and uniforms, etc and told him it would be about $500. This time with tears running down his cheeks he reached once again into the file folder took out another envelope. In it was $500 in cash. He said to me, "While I was shaving this morning the Lord said to me give him $500 more!"

"Come and listen you that fear the Lord and let me tell you what He has done for me!"

Call to Me, and I will answer you, and show you great and mighty things, which you do not know.'

"My God shall supply all your need according to His riches in glory by Christ Jesus."

Breathless!

In the middle of 1981, I received a most unusual letter. The letter came from the Congress of the United States of America inviting me to the 1982 Presidential Prayer Breakfast in Washington, USA, in February 1982. I felt for sure that this was a mistake, and that this letter was intended for my brother, Dr. Neville Gallimore then a Cabinet Minister of the Jamaica Government, as in my mind there was no way that my name could have come up for such an invitation. I took the letter to my brother Neville. He looked at it and said, "My name is not Gerry Gallimore. I am not the leader of Jamaica YFC, nor is this my address. This is clearly an invitation to you Gerry."

I discussed it with my Board and YFCI leaders and they all felt it was a signal honor and that I should do everything possible to attend. The next big hurdle was to secure a ticket to Washington. Jamaica YFC had no money to provide this ticket. By faith I went down to Allied Travel Service, the travel agency I always used for any overseas travel, showed them the letter of invitation and explained my dilemma. Mrs. Blake, who headed the travel agency, agreed that it was a signal honor to be invited and said she would provide the ticket on a pay later basis. I was most grateful for this facilitation and gave the Lord thanks right there.

I arrived in Washington on the eve of the Presidential Prayer Breakfast and was picked up at the airport by my wife's cousin, Ruby who drove me to the Washington Hilton Hotel where the breakfast would be held the following morning. There was a long line of folks checking in, and then it was my turn. I showed the clerk of the reception the letter from the U.S. Congress and she checked to confirm that my name was on the list…and it was. And then she asked me for a credit card to cover the expenses. I did not have a credit card. In fact I had never heard of such a thing as a credit card up to that point in my life. With a letter of invitation from the US Congress it had never occurred to me that I would need to cover any expenses associated with the breakfast, feeling sure that this was taken care of by the invitation. I said this to the clerk who then went to make another check but came back to me and said, "Sorry Mr. Gallimore we will need a credit card in order to confirm this reservation." I stood there bewildered. A sense of panic hit me as I had no money and no means to pay for the hotel. I could not even ask how much it would be.

In the midst of my panic someone tapped me on the shoulder and I turned around to see Dr. Sam Wolgemuth, the President of Youth For Christ international standing behind me. He greeted me warmly and said, "Is there a problem?" I told him my predicament. He said, "No problem – you can stay with me. I have a suite in the hotel and my wife Grace could not come at the last minute. You can stay with me." I shared the luxury of a two-bedroom suite and attended the Presidential Breakfast addressed by President Ronald Reagan giving his moving testimony following on the assassination attempt on his life.

"Come and listen you that fear the Lord and let me tell you what He has done for me!"

"Call to Me, and I will answer you, and show you great and mighty things, which you do not know."

"My God shall supply all your need according to His riches in glory by Christ Jesus."
Hallelujah!!!

Benefit

"Faithful is He who calls you." 1Thes. 5:24

After serving 16+ years as National Director of Jamaica YFC, 6 years of which I also served as Regional Director for Caribbean Youth For Christ, in 1984 I was appointed Area Director for The Americas – one of five World Areas established by Youth For Christ International with Head Office in Singapore. This YFCI/Americas World Area comprised YFC ministries in 22 countries inclusive of – USA, Canada, Central and South America, and the Caribbean. (I was succeeded at Jamaica YFC by Dexter Gordon, an experienced YFC leader, graduate of Jamaica Theological Seminary – a gifted young man with a keen mind who had previously served with me in Jamaica YFC leadership.)

I opened the YFCI/the Americas Area Office in Cross Roads (Kingston, Jamaica) in 1984. In the face of this enormous Area responsibility one of the first things I did was to pull together 22 believers to form an America's Area Prayer Group to provide prayer support for me and my family, as well as praying for YFC ministry in the Area. In addition each member of that Prayer Group was assigned responsibility to pray for a specific country within the Area.

On taking up this challenging assignment I felt the need for additional training to better equip myself to fulfill the new responsibilities. With the blessing and approval of the President of YFCI, Rev. Jim Groen (Denver, USA) and that of the General Director of YFCI, Rev. Jim Wilson (YFCI Head Office, Singapore) I enrolled in an MA program at Denver Seminary in Denver Colorado in 1984. This was an intense summer program designed for working Christian leaders to complete the MA program over four summers. This meant I would be leaving Sonia and our three children for that period of time each year. Another venture of faith for travel expenses, tuition fees, housing and food, etc. all I will say at this point is that the Lord provided for each of those four summers. Praise His Name!

While at seminary in summer of 1984 one day at a lunch time we had an informal address by one Rev. Fred Nofer, a retired Presbyterian minister representing the Presbyterian Ministerial Fund. He shared the importance of financial preparation for retirement citing the plight of many aging Christian workers who for one reason or the other arrived at old age with no such preparation. He then explained that the Presbyterian Ministerial Fund had been established with this objective in mind and encouraged all of us to consider a mutual fund like the PMF.

I was 46 years old at the time and sensed the wisdom of Fred's presentation and the urgency of doing something notwithstanding the seriousness of my everyday challenges. I had a private talk with Fred thanking him for his on target presentation. I outlined my living by faith situation and the two major problems of not having money to open an account with PMF, and further that by law I could not send money out of Jamaica to support such an account.

Fred was most understanding of my situation. He surprised me by advising that if I had even as little as $50 I could open an account with PMF. He further said I could use his home address in Denver so that no statements or communication would come to me in Jamaica, and that when I returned to Denver he would update me on the account. I took the forms from him and when I was leaving seminary that summer I had enough to open the account, with the understanding that my only other contributions would be whatever money I happened to have at the end of each summer. And so it was that whatever I had left over at the

end of each summer I would leave with Fred for
that account.

Little did I know at that time how significant a
blessing this would be and how faithful a
brother Fred Nofer would prove to be!

Brother

"My God shall supply all your need according to His riches in glory by Christ Jesus."   Phil. 4:19

Believe it!   Yes! Yes – God can do what Philippians 4:19 affirms!

The job of being Area Director for the Americas involved considerable travel to the 22 countries. Apart from plane connections to USA, Canada and some of the islands in the Caribbean, all travel to Central and South America meant flying to Miami in order to make connections. The YFC International Head Office in Singapore kept pressing me to relocate to Miami so as to better serve the Area. However, both Sonia and I were deeply committed to Jamaica and involved in various aspects of Christian witness in the nation, and so did not accommodate this option.

Things changed however in 1988. Our first daughter Trudy started attending university in Miami. The Lord provided a dear friend who made accommodation available to Trudy. That same year my younger brother Rupert and his wife Eva decided to send their daughter Cheryl to university in Miami. As parents we agreed that it would be good for Trudy and Cheryl to be together.

On one of my trips from South America I had a few hours stopover in Miami which I used to explore with Trudy various accommodation possibilities for herself and Cheryl. After about two hours it was time for me to make my way back to the airport to catch my flight to Jamaica. As Trudy and I were driving to the airport we passed through Pembroke Pines (then sparsely populated). We passed by a location with about 2 dozen or more flags of different colors waving in the breeze. I asked Trudy what that meant, since back in Jamaica those kinds of flags usually indicated location of a 'balmyard' (obeah/voodoo). She told me it was advertisement for a housing development. I had about 15 minutes to spare and she said to me, "Daddy, you want to take a look?"
We stopped out of curiosity. Someone from the sales office on the compound showed us through 4 single-family display units – one (1) 4-bedroom and three (3) 3-bedroom units. When we completed the tour Trudy got real excited and said, "Daddy, what if you and Uncle Rupert could combine together to pay down on one of these units so that Cheryl and I and if others of our siblings come to school here in Miami, we could all be together. Instead of paying rent you

and Uncle Rupert would be paying about the same amount of money for mortgage, and then eventually when we are finished school you both could sell back the unit and recover what you would have lost in paying rental!"

The thought made sense. Back in the sales office I inquired what would be the down payment on the least expensive of the units. I was totally blown away when I was told, "You can pay down $500 to secure a unit for two weeks. If at the end of that time you decide to go ahead with the purchase, we will ask you to put down 5% of the purchase price if you are an American citizen or a green card holder. If not, we require a 10% deposit. If we don't hear from you within the two weeks you will forfeit this down payment. But if we hear from you within two weeks the down payment can be refunded or become a part of the required down payment " These figures blew me away because in Jamaica the down payment requirement was 30%. I got excited, and asked when did they expect to have the last set of units ready for occupancy? I was told in about 12 months time. I asked to be shown the map and shown where on the map the last set of units would be built. By faith I asked that my name be put on one of those last units to be built.

I took out my checkbook and wrote them a

check for $500!

I had stepped out in faith once again! It was a heady feeling. My daughter Trudy was elated. We could hardly believe all that had transpired in the space of just about 30 minutes! She drove me to the airport and I caught my flight to Jamaica. I could hardly wait to tell Sonia the exciting news of what we had done.

She was not excited. "You did what? You did what? You paid down on a house without discussing it with me? You paid down on a house that I have not seen??" She was as mad as a hatter. "I can't believe it – I can't believe what you have done! And I know I will neither like the model you have chosen nor the location where it will be built."

I could not appease her. She immediately went to the phone and called Trudy with the strongest reprimand, "How could you allow your father to do something like this..." and she carried on. Of our three children, Trudy was perceived as the 'sophisticat.' Trudy said, "Mommy, you will love it" and proceeded with excitement to describe the unit and her strong support from what I had done. At the end of the phone call Sonia said, "Well if Trudy says I would like it, then I will wait and see." With that the atmosphere eased considerably.

That Christmas instead of bringing Trudy home to Jamaica, Sonia insisted that she wanted to go to Florida to see for herself what I had done. We arrived in Florida and we went to the housing location—"PIERPOINTE" on Johnson Street. She insisted that she did not want to know which of the four display units we had reserved as she wanted to make her own choice. Trudy and I kept quiet as we went through the units. She selected model C which was the very model Trudy and I had reserved.

By the end of 1988 with two of our girls at school in Florida and with my extensive overseas travel Sonia began to feel the loneliness of an 'empty nest.' On one of my trips to South America Sonia came down with an acute appendicitis requiring immediate surgery. Unfortunately, I had our health insurance card with me. This was a problem. It was further complicated by the fact that the doctor and hospital both needed my signature before they would proceed with the surgery. Thankfully, my brother, Dr. Neville Gallimore, a medical doctor and the then Minister of Health intervened and gave permission on my behalf for the surgery to be done. When I returned home from that trip the first words that my wife Sonia said to me was, "You can no longer leave me alone for these long trips. You must either ask the Lord for a new assignment or I move to Florida so I can be with the girls."

This was a major decision for my wife since she was so passionately involved with social work among our marginalized underprivileged folks. With the call of God strong upon our hearts after much prayer we started to explore the possibility of relocating to Florida.

The Youth For Christ International Office was delighted to hear this as in their view Florida was the logical gateway from which to serve the Americas Area. With the facilitation of the YFCI Office we made application to the US Embassy for 'green cards' in order to move residency to Florida.

Right about this time we were advised by the PIERPOINTE Housing project in Florida that our house was near completion and that we needed to come in with the 10% down payment and to sign the various documents.

In one sense this was great news. Sonia and I stood amazed at the Lord's timing. We were moving to Florida – just waiting on our green card approval, and to hear that the Pierpointe house would likely be ready by the time we arrived. We could not miss the hand of our Father! When I paid down on this project (see chapter 7) I had absolutely no idea, no concept,

51

no plan about moving to the USA. But Father knew!

"For I know the plans I have for you," declares the Lord, "plans to prosper you and not to harm you, plans to give you hope and a future."
(Jer. 29:11 –NIV)

In another sense this news was a reality check. In a few days time we would need to have US $8000 to satisfy the 10% deposit. We turned to the Lord out of habit and out of necessity. After prayer I called Fred Nofer in Denver and shared with him all that had developed. I said to him, "Fred, I know when I opened that account with you it was to help prepare for old-age and retirement. But in the light of this development I am going to need whatever you have to help with this down payment, so I have to ask how much money is available in that account?" You can imagine the jumping up and hallelujahs that went up from Sonia and I when Fred said, "You have about $8000 in the account!" I said out loud, "there is no way that it can be $8000 considering the small amounts of my contribution?" Fred told me the fund had done very well. I thanked him profusely and asked him to send me a check for the total sum. With the $500 I had paid down a year before, _we had the required down payment._ The housing project sent the documents to us in

Jamaica by FedEx. Sonia and I signed the documents returning them with the check for $8000!! Yea....

"Come and listen you that fear the Lord and let me tell you what He has done for me!"
He supplies *"all our needs according to His riches in glory by Christ Jesus."*

Our application for US residency (green cards) came through and on May 24, 1989 we arrived in Florida. On that very day the builders completed the house in Pierpointe and we took delivery the following day, May 25, 1989. <u>God's amazing timing!</u> Forgive me when I shout once again with the Psalmist:
"Come and listen you that fear the Lord and let me tell you what He has done for me!"

But that was not all!

More blessings!

Shortly before leaving Jamaica for Florida I had a call from YFCI General Director Jim Wilson (a Canadian) telling me that one of his close friends was selling a fully furnished 2-bedroom apartment in Boca Raton, Florida! His friend expected to sell it fully furnished but the buyer had informed him that he did not want the furnishings and the place had to be handed over totally empty in 10 days time. Jim's friend had a problem – how to dispose of everything in the apartment within 10 days. Jim called me to say, "Gerry provided you can have the place totally empty within 10 days you can take everything that is in the apartment." I excitedly agreed and immediately called the Fort Lauderdale Youth For Christ Director, shared the development and asked for his help. He very kindly agreed to help and said he would put the things in storage until we arrived.

When we arrived in Florida we found just about everything that we needed for our new house! We got…
… *a living room suite,*
… *dining table and chairs,*
… *pots, fry pans, cutlery, crockery;*

... beds, vanities, chests of drawers;
... linen, towels; vacuum-cleaner, brooms; etc, etc!!!!

These items were all in excellent condition. All
provided by the mighty hand of God.

You will have to bear with me when I keep on
shouting His praise and invite...

*"You that fear the Lord to listen and let me tell you
what He has done for me!"*

As I write this we have continued to live in that
same house for these last 31 years. After 31
years we still have the same bedroom suite in
our master bedroom, the same dining table and
chairs, the same china closet in the kitchen.

The Lord is good! Yes!! We cannot help but
shout His praise and join the Psalmist in
testifying of His great goodness toward us.

This is what Father still says to you and to me...
*"Call to Me, and I will answer you, and show you
great and mighty things, which you do not know."*
(Jer. 33:3)
You of like faith...praise Him with us for His
mighty deeds!

Unexpected Development

I served as the YFCI/America's Area Director from 1984 – 1990. From 1984 – 1989 my office was in Kingston, Jamaica, from which location I traveled to and serviced the 22 countries in my portfolio. During that time, I spent the summers of 1984 – 1988 at Denver Seminary in Denver, Colorado pursuing an MA in theology/Youth Ministry. I found that program under the tutelage of godly, learned professors to be extremely beneficial, enlightening and instructive, equipping me for more effective ministry. The then President of YFCI/Chairman of the Board, Rev. Jim Groen and his wife Dotti live in Denver. Jim and Dotti were my family away from home, providing me with warm fellowship and caring support during my time in Denver. I am forever grateful. *(Thanks and blessings on you both – Jim and Dotti!)*

The world family of YFC ministries come together for a major YFC International Convocation once every three years. This Convocation is an important time of worldwide ministry review, reports, training, inspiration, forward planning and decision-making.

The YFCI World Leadership Team comprising the 5 Area Directors (Americas, Africa, Asia, Europe, Middle East) and the international staff meets every six months in conjunction with the YFCI Board meeting to facilitate reporting to the Board.

At such a meeting in San Antonio, Texas in 1989 I was absolutely blown away when my name was proposed by the Board's Search Committee as their nominee to become the next President of YFCI, to be voted on at the YFCI Convocation scheduled for Nairobi, Kenya in July 1990.

I was frightened. I felt inadequate and unready.

Why me – when there were others whom I felt were more ready, more experienced and more capable than me. I needed time to seek the Lord – to think and pray this through. I asked the Prayer Group in Jamaica (chapter 6) to intercede with me for guidance as to whether to allow my name to go forward. The size of the challenge loomed heavily for me. I come from the little island of Jamaica. While well-known in Jamaica and the Caribbean community, I was an almost unknown entity in the important world areas of North America, Europe, Asia, Africa and Australia. To provide ministry leadership at that level, to be responsible for the vision and the resources necessary, were scary indeed.

After three months of much prayer and consultation with trusted brethren, I felt God's peace in allowing my name to go forward.

My wife Sonia accompanied me to that YFC International Convocation in Nairobi, Kenya in July 1990. In the last session of the last day of the General Assembly my nomination was presented to the floor for secret voting as required by the YFCI Constitution. When the matter was put to the delegates they all rose in unanimous applause and I was elected by consensus instead of by ballot. In that same Convocation the General Assembly voted to combine the titles of "President" and "General Director" (eliminating confusion as to who was the real leader of the organization) into one new title of "President/CEO" which title was conferred on me. My term of office would be for three years in the first place.

In that election I became the first non-white, non-American, Third World person to become President/CEO of Youth For Christ International.

I felt like David standing before Goliath with only a sling in my hand. But like David I too can shout, *"Come and listen you that fear the Lord and let me tell you what He has done for me!"*

At that time the Head Office of YFCI was in Singapore. It was required that the President/CEO operate from the Head Office, to which location Sonia and I would spend the next six years. We left our home and children in Florida and moved to Singapore, exactly half a world away. Singapore is a beautiful, highly developed, first world little island with one of the lowest crime rates in the world. We loved it! Sonia and I made some great friends there – Sonia more so than me. Her friendships have been maintained over all these 24 years since we left Singapore.

I served two 3-year terms (6 years) as the President/CEO of YFCI. They were demanding years – providing vision, leadership, resources and strategic direction to YFC ministries in over 120 countries. Of course I could not/did not do this alone. I remain deeply indebted to the Board of YFCI, to the Singapore Head Office staff, to the World Leadership Team, to a few consultants and to the prayer team that undergirded us.

As I think back on all the responsibilities, the challenges, the extensive travel and the seemingly impossible demands of leadership at that level over those 6 years, all I can say is that like Peter <u>the Lord enabled me to walk on water</u>!

I can't help it; I have to join David in what I believe he must have said when with only a sling and a stone he was able to bring down the giant Goliath. I think I hear David shouting, *"Come and listen all you who fear God and let me tell you what Yahweh…what El Shaddai has done for me."* The Lord…yes, **the Lord** has done **great things** for which I shout His praises! (Ps. 126:3)

We look on in amazement at what the Lord can do with the little – the two fish and five loaves – that we put in His hands.

Visit to China

In 1991 Rev. Werner Burklin (see Chapter 1) who
by this time had retired from YFC International
and established a ministry called Werner Burklin
Ministries, invited me, along with four other
Christian leaders, to accompany him on a
missions trip to Nanjing, China to do a one-week
training program with pastors in evangelism.
Werner had cleared this program with Bishop
Ting, the head of the China Christian Council.
We all needed to get visas to enter China. Since
'teaching evangelism' would not qualify for a
visa, our visit would include some touring of the
Nanjing area allowing us to apply for a tourist
visa.

I applied to the Chinese Embassy in USA some
three months in advance of the mission date and
received my entry visa.

The team consisting of 2 Germans (Werner
Burklin and son Eric Burklin), 2 Americans (Bill
Weldon & soloist Ed Lyman), 1 New Zealander
(Wilbur Wright) and 1 Jamaican (me) met in
Hong Kong and together we took a flight to
Nanjing. There were severe weather problems
that day in Nanjing with the result that our flight

was diverted to Shanghai. We would have to travel by rail from Shanghai to Nanjing.

The six of us approached the immigration officer. I was the last of the six. The other five were processed without any problem and now it was my turn to hand in my passport opened at the visa. I froze as the immigration officer in a stern voice accused me of trying to enter China without a visa! I said to the officer, "I do have a visa" and pointed to the page that was open in front of him. With a stern authoritative voice he repeated that I was attempting to enter China without a visa. I was fearful and confused and once again pointed to the visa. He said, "Visa expired. Expired visa – no visa!" I was dumbfounded. I had applied to the Chinese Embassy for a visa indicating the date for my visit to China. The visa was all in Chinese. Having received the visa (stamped in my passport) I was sure that all was well.

The officer took me into a small room and started to grill me accusingly about the purpose for my visit to China. "If you are tourist why you not visit Shanghai or some other city? Why Nanjing?" The officer was clearly very suspicious. Prior to the trip we had all been warned not to mention the evangelism aspect of our mission. Christians in communist China had been persecuted for their faith for 30+ years.

To mention "evangelism" would have been a no-no for a foreigner seeking entry.

The hostile manner in which the officer grilled me caused me to begin to fear that I might end up in detention. Under questioning I mentioned that there were five others of us in the group. The officer wanted to know their nationalities. when I mentioned that two of them were Americans, he immediately wanted to know their names. He then left me alone in the room to further interrogate the Americans.

As you can imagine in my spirit I was crying out to the Lord through the whole of this frightening experience. When the officer left me alone in the room I cried out to the Lord in deeper desperation asking for His intervention. You have to forgive me, but when I am under pressure like this my prayer is sometimes just one word – "Jesus! Jesus! Jesus!" It was one of those times that we find in Romans 8:26, ***"We do not know how to pray as we should, but the Spirit Himself intercedes for us with <u>groanings too deep for words.</u>"***

After a while the Immigration Officer returned to the room with a form in his hand and he said to me, "You very lucky man – first time we give visa here in Shanghai." And he handed me the form to fill out.

Hallelujah! Hallelujah!

When there seemed to be no way, the Lord made a way for me.

He stood over me as I filled out the form. And then I froze – for there was a question asking, "What organization do you represent?" I knew immediately that if I put "Youth For Christ International" it would have been over – the organizational name would have given me away.

But I am a servant of the Lord. I must be truthful. I wrote, "YFCI."

He never asked what "YFCI" stood for. I was admitted to China, went by rail with the team to Nanjing and fulfilled our mission.

There were 80 seminar participants from 10 different provinces – all eager to know more about the Bible and about the subject of evangelism. They took copious notes. At the close of our 10 day seminar Werner Burklin presented each participant with a set of basic theological books. The mission was a success and was to become the basis of many such teaching missions to church leaders in China by Werner Burklin Ministries, (now, China Partners).

When I arrived back in Singapore I got a phone call from my brother Rupert in Kingston Jamaica. We exchanged greetings and then Rupert said to me, "Your prayer group here (see chapter 6) met on the day you were going into China to pray God's blessing on your travel and on your ministry. While they were praying Winston McKay suddenly interrupted the group and said to them, I sense that Bro. Gerry is in trouble and we need to pray for God's intervention." Then Rupert asked me, "Was there any problem?" With the blessing of heaven running like rivers over my soul I shared with Rupert what had happened. My brothers and sisters, from half a world away this spiritual battle was fought and won! Once again I felt like David of old when he said:

"Come and listen all you who fear God and let me tell you what the Lord has done for me!"

Yes! Yes! The Lord has done marvelous things for me for which I can't help but shout His praises!

Clothes

In my role as President/CEO of Youth For
Christ International I traveled extensively from
my base in Singapore. In 1993 on one of my
trips to New York I was invited to speak at
Bronx Bethany Church of the Nazarene pastored
by my dear friend Dr. Seymour Cole.

In the audience that night were three dear
Jamaican friends, Karl McGrath, Marie Dalton
and Lubric Johnson. At the end of the service
they invited me to go with them. My
presumption was one of our usual fellowship
chats over ice cream. Instead they took me to a
men's shop as they wanted to give me the gift of
a suit. They convinced me that every preacher
needs a black suit and so a black suit it would
be.

As we moved along in the store looking for the
black suit I saw a grey pinstriped suit and tried
on the jacket. It complimented my graying hair.
I put it back on the rack and soon we found the
black suit. I noticed the price tag on the black
suit was way beyond a price I was comfortable
with but said nothing since they also saw the
price and seemed very comfortable with it. To

my great surprise they also picked up the grey pinstriped suit that I had tried on earlier. At this I protested strongly knowing that they were just working folks not flush with money, but they assured me that there was a 50% discount on the suits and they overrode my objection.

I was still very uncomfortable as they came to the checkout counter. I remembered then that on entering the store there was a display of cheap suits at $50 each, and so I quickly went to that rack and picked up two cheap suits totaling $100, rushed to the checkout counter and said to them, "I am not comfortable with the cost of the two suits you have selected, buy these two instead." I thought I had made my point and was beginning to feel comfortable again. I was utterly flabbergasted when they paid for the 4 suits saying that in my role as the head of YFCI and as a preacher, I would need them.

I got very quiet as we stepped out of the store working through the emotions of surprise, thanksgiving and almost a sense of embarrassment because it seemed too much. We got back into the car and they said, "But Gerry, how are you going to go home with four suits for yourself and without an outfit for your wife?" I protested vehemently feeling that they had already spent too much money. However they took me to another store and bought an outfit for my wife. Earlier that evening I had been boasting off as grandparents do about our first grandchild, showing them photos of this granddaughter. They blew me away when on top of everything they bought a beautiful outfit for our 2+ year-old granddaughter Gabrielle!

4 suits, 1 outfit for my wife and 1 outfit for my granddaughter…all at one time!! I could not have bought any of these on my own…*but the Lord provided*!!   You can understand why I feel like David back in Psalm 66:16 when he said:

"Come and listen you that fear the Lord and let me tell you what He has done for me!"

I join with the Apostle Paul in testifying as he did in Philippians 4:19:

"My God shall supply all your needs according to His riches in glory by Christ Jesus."

He is a good God. He is a loving Father who surprises us from time to time with unexpected gifts. 28 years later as I write this I still have those four suits. I wear the black suit to every funeral I attend and on many other preaching or formal occasions, and I have left instructions to be buried in that black suit when God calls me home. Thanks once again to Karl, Marie and to Lubric.

Others of you who read this testimony will wonder if I have forgotten or if I don't equally appreciate the gifts of other suits, shirts, shoes, Bibles, Bible covers, groceries, cooked meals, money, car repairs (and the list goes on) that you have given me. I will probably embarrass myself if I try to list all your names; and some of you would prefer to keep your benevolence private. Let me assure each one of you that I have <u>not</u> forgotten any of the hands that my Father has used to be a blessing to Sonia, to our family and to me.

Let me say thanks once again! Every day in our family devotions in faith we pray to the Father, ***"Give us this day our daily bread"*** and then we watch to see how He answers our prayer.

He has faithfully provided over these past 52 years.

Tomorrow we will once again follow His instruction in Matthew 6:11 and ask Him to, *"Give us this day our daily bread."* We have His Word. We wait to see how and by whom He provides!

Lost in Ukraine

In 1994 while serving as President of Youth For Christ International (and residing in Singapore) I was invited by the Youth Arm of the Ukraine Baptist Fellowship to speak at the Ukraine Baptist Youth Convention being held in Kiev, Ukraine. Given the communist suppression of religion, this was the first time for a long time that such a convention was being held in Ukraine itself. (They previously met for their convention in other countries.)

This visit was quite an eye-opener in many ways. Coming as I do from the little island of Jamaica we have no doubt that everything European is way in advance of Jamaica! I was shocked to find that the airport in Kiev was considerably below the standard of our Jamaican airports. The young man that collected me from the airport and drove an old Volkswagen car that I had to help push in order to get it started. I arrived at the Convention site after the evening meal and was taken to where I would sleep for the next 6 days. As the invited speaker for the convention I assumed I would be in a room by myself. I was taken aback when I realized I would be sharing the room with three young men, all in their early twenties. Fortunately these young men were Ukrainian-Americans and spoke English. They had left a bed for me near to the bathroom door. I very soon realized why they had avoided that bed – there was a smell coming from the bathroom! The water from the pipe in the bathroom was discolored. There was no toilet paper. There was a bathtub but no shower. No soap. No towels.

I asked the fellows about toilet paper. "Did you not bring toilet paper?"

I asked them about towels. "Did you not bring your own towels?" I told him no. They then said to me that they were advised to bring all these items as they would not be available here at the accommodation. I had not received that memo! One of the fellows offered me a bar of soap and another one loaned me a towel. I asked about drinking water and one of them kindly offered me a bottle.

By now I was very hungry and said to them is there a restaurant nearby to which I could go to get a meal? They advised me that they were not aware of any nearby restaurants and the other problem would be transport to get to such a restaurant. My immediate response was surely somebody here has a car and would facilitate me." They smiled and told me they had not seen any cars on the compound. Thankfully they took me to the dining room, explained who I was and that I was hungry. I was given something to eat.

To say the least, this was a difficult start. I am by nature a very private person – I close the door even if I am only going to change my mind. I was not very comfortable with unexpectedly having to share a room with three young strangers.

By the grace of God I made it through the end of the Convention.

I was down to speak at a Baptist Church in Kiev the following Sunday, with the understanding that I would be accommodated by the pastor of the church who would then take me on the Monday to meet with Youth Leader of the Ukrainian Baptist Convention. I was to return to Singapore the following Tuesday.

I was dropped off at the Baptist Church and was immediately met by a tall Ukrainian young man (whose name I have forgotten) who introduced himself and said he would be my translator. He spoke English fluently and interpreted for me as the church service progressed.

The chapel was packed. My interpreter explained that with the fall of communism Christians who had been repressed in expressing their faith now flocked to the churches rejoicing in the newfound freedom to worship.

It came time in the service for the sermon and I immediately assumed they would be calling on me, but to my surprise they called another preacher who spoke for approximately 30 minutes. My interpreter explained that there were usually several speakers. The service went on for a long time with another three or four sermons. I begun to conclude that maybe all I would be expected to do was to say a few words about Youth For Christ, as in my mind these people could never survive another sermon!

The pastor called my name and my translator made it clear that I was just announced as the main speaker for the morning and that a full sermon was expected. I went to the pulpit and delivered what the Lord had laid on my heart. Speaking through a translator is sometimes difficult and awkward, but this translator was proficient which made all the difference.

The service was over and the folks began to disperse. My translator sat with me as I waited for the pastor who was to provide me with

accommodation for the next two days.
My translator said to me that there was a
problem as he could hear the pastor checking
with various persons as to whether they could
accommodate me. He then said to me I will take
care of you at my place, and immediately went
and spoke with the pastor. This relieved an
awkward situation. We left to take public
transportation to his apartment.

At the Youth Convention I had eaten the same
meal three times per day for six days. I was
hungry after the church service and was anxious
to get to a restaurant to have a change of menu.
I suggested this to my translator but he
immediately dismissed it. The cost of a
restaurant meal in his view would be too
expensive. I assured him I would cover the cost
but he told me not to worry he would prepare
something for me at his apartment.

After about 45 minutes we arrived at his
apartment. He lived on the 18th floor. There is
no elevator in this building! I had my luggage
with me. He very kindly offered to carry the
luggage. I had a hard time keeping up with him
going up those endless steps. The apartment
was very small – 2 bedrooms, one bathroom, one
kitchen and a small living area. His dad in
underwear was sleeping on a couch in the
living area. His mom and sister were away for

the weekend and he ushered me into their room to rest while he prepared the meal. He brought in my luggage and warned me not to leave it unlocked since his father was an alcoholic and would likely search my luggage looking for money to support his habit.

There were two unmade single beds in the room. I took that in stride since they were not expecting to have a visitor. I tried to make myself comfortable, concerned about where I would sleep and how things would be for the next two days. I fell asleep.

He woke me up to a meal of boiled potatoes and frankfurters. By this time I was very hungry and thoroughly enjoyed the change of menu. I spent the rest of the afternoon preparing to speak at another Baptist Church that night. I suggested we call a taxi for transport to the church but again he felt that would cost too much. We took public transport.

Like at the morning service the attendance was very good. This time there were only two speakers ahead of me. When the church service was over I was again hungry and this time I insisted that we go to a restaurant. He yielded and we went to a restaurant at a small hotel. We enjoyed a great meal of goulash and boiled potatoes. Still concerned about where I would be sleeping and how comfortable it would be, I asked my translator about how much per night for the hotel as I was very concerned about inconveniencing him and his family with my unexpected visits. He said the cost would be about US$40 per night. I immediately suggested going back to his apartment collecting my luggage and returning to check-in at the hotel so as to be out of his hair. He strongly objected saying that the cost of the hotel for the two nights would be more than the salary he made for a month. Not to worry, he would have me sleep in his bedroom. That settled that and we returned to his apartment.

I had a good night sleep, but the bathroom was a challenge.

At about 10 a.m. on that Monday morning he took me to the Ukrainian Baptist Convention office where I was to meet with the denomination's youth leader. He introduced me to the staff and I was given a seat to await the arrival of the youth leader. Up to sometime after midday the youth leader had not arrived. No one in the office spoke English. Beginning to feel hungry I decided I would go to look for a cafeteria, restaurant – anyplace I could get a snack. I tried as best I could to indicate to the receptionist that I was going for a walk and would soon be back.

I came out of the office and made strong mental note of where it was located intending to simply walk down the street and look for a place to eat and then to make my way back. I walked on and on and on but saw no sign of an eating place. By this time I am very hungry. The only place I knew of where I could get food was where I had eaten the night before at the hotel. I hailed a taxi and asked him to take me there – which he did.

I went into the restaurant and once again had a satisfying meal of boiled potatoes and goulash. Now I was anxious to get back to the Baptist Headquarters. I went to the receptionist at the hotel and asked if they could call a taxi for me to take me to the Baptist headquarters. The young lady immediately asked if I knew the phone number for the Baptist Office. I said no but asked if she would check the telephone directory. I could not believe my ears when she said, "We do not have a telephone directory!"

I was flabbergasted. Coming as I do from the little Third World country called Jamaica it is unthinkable to us at anywhere in Europe would be short of such a basic commodity. I shuddered as I realized that I did not know the address, nor have a phone number for the Baptist Office, nor did I have an address or phone number for my translator who was due to collect me from the

Baptist Office at 4.00p.m. that afternoon. It is now minutes to 3.00p.m. My luggage, my passport and ticket back to Singapore are all at my translator's apartment.

I am lost! I am booked with a nonrefundable ticket to fly back to Singapore at 9.00am the following morning.

I am beginning to feel a sense of panic. My translator will go to the Baptist Office at four p.m. and will not find me, and no one at the office will have any idea of where I am. It was futile asking for a taxi as I would not be able to tell the taxi driver the address of either the Baptist Office or the apartment where I am staying!! My sense of lostness is intensifying. How could this happen to me – I have traveled the world (over 90 countries) and here I am lost in Ukraine.

When something like this happens there is only one thing to do. I sat down and cried to the Lord. If ever I needed a miracle it was then. 4.00pm came. In my mind's eye I saw my translator turning up at the Baptist Office and not finding me.

I prayed. I prayed anxiously. I prayed. As the time passed I got increasingly anxious.

I could hardly believe my eyes when somewhere about 5:30pm I saw my translator walk through the door!

"Come and listen you that fear the Lord and let me tell you what He has done for me!" Hallelujah! Hallelujah!

How did he find me? He said he went to the Baptist Office at 4.00pm. The Baptist Youth Leader had not come to the office. No one there had any idea what had become of me except to tell him I had left the office around lunchtime. He said at that point he concluded that I had gone to find something to eat and he knew that the only place I knew about in Kiev was the restaurant we had eaten the night before. He was aware I did not have the address for his apartment, and so he decided that the hotel was the only clue he had to follow.

Needless to say I was overjoyed to see him. God had come to my rescue and answered my prayer once again. I can't keep quiet – I can't keep it all to myself. Like David I feel constrained to say, *"Come and listen you that fear the Lord and let me tell you what He has done for me!"*

He hears 'lost' sheep when we cry for His help. My translator took me to the airport the following morning. I caught my 9.00am flight back to Singapore. Thanks be to God!

Big... Yes, Big indeed!

"Amsterdam 2000," Conference of Preaching Evangelists convened by famed evangelist Dr. Billy Graham will go down in history as perhaps the largest event bringing together evangelists from around the world. Some have called it, "the most internationally representative gathering ever" bringing together more than 11,000 Conference participants from some 215 countries and territories. The venue – Amsterdam; the dates July 29 – August 6, 2000.

This conference would draw together from around the world, leading evangelists, lesser-known evangelists, top church leaders, leading theologians and prominent evangelism professors. The purpose of this conference – to inspire and equip evangelists to use effective ways to present the Gospel in the 21st century. *Amsterdam 2000* would be a legacy of the man God used to become the most renowned evangelist (perhaps of all time), Dr. Billy Graham – to pass on the torch of evangelism to leaders around the world.

I couldn't believe it when I was invited to be a plenary speaker at this auspicious event!

I had had the privilege of attending the Lausanne Congress on World Evangelization held in Amsterdam in 1974. I had also had the privilege of attending the Pattaya Conference on Evangelization held in Thailand in 1980. At each of those conferences the platform speakers were all renowned, distinguished, accredited speakers in their field. We drank in the information, the inspiration and the challenges that they shared. Never at any time did it ever even cross my mind of being anything but an attendee at conferences like these.

I was blown away when somewhere towards the end of 1999/beginning of the year 2000 I received a phone call from Las Newman of Jamaica telling me about *Amsterdam 2000* and that an Executive of the *Amsterdam 2000* Organizing Committee was in Jamaica promoting the attendance of Caribbean participants in the Amsterdam 2000 conference. Las then told me that the leaders who met with this Executive convinced him that given the strength and influence of the church within the Caribbean there should be a speaker from the Caribbean at the *Amsterdam 2000* conference. The Executive agreed to relay this request to the Program Committee. Las then blew me away when he said that they had unanimously agreed that "You, Gerry Gallimore, should be that speaker." I immediately declined.

In the words of a renowned President of the USA, I felt such an assignment was "above my pay grade." I immediately reflected on my experience at the Lausanne Conference in 1974 and the Pattaya Conference in 1980 and knew it was beyond me. Despite Las Newman's strong appeal, I told him no.

I was terrified at the request and relieved that I had declined.

A few minutes later a call came in from my dear friend and respected Christian brother from Jamaica, Robert Levy. Robert came on in the strongest terms telling me that I could not say no to this request because the leaders in Jamaica had come on too strong to the representative from *Amsterdam 2000* about a speaker from the Caribbean region, and had all assured him that I would fill the slot. Robert said, "You cannot let us down Gerry – we know you can do it. Be assured of the full prayer backing of all of us in the Caribbean – but you must say yes." Robert waited for my response. I heard myself telling him that I would attempt it. Robert was relieved and said he would relay my decision to the rest of the brethren.

Within days I had communication from the *Amsterdam 2000* Planning Committee confirming my role and giving me the assignment to be a Plenary Speaker on the subject, *"The Evangelist Communicates Effectively."*

I felt terrified! Me, a little Third World servant from the island of Jamaica to be a plenary speaker at a conference like this – alongside of renowned distinguished leaders like Billy Kim, J. I. Packer, Ravi Zacharias, John Stott, Annie Graham-Lotz, Archbishop George Carey, Åjith Fernando, Bill Bright, Chuck Colson, Stephen Olford and Franklin Graham, to name a few.

Had I allowed myself to take on more than I could handle?

I asked my prayer team in Jamaica for prayer support. I sought the Lord for a Word. I put in the time for research, study and preparation. Added to those tensions was the fact that I was under a time constraint. The Organizing Committee gave a deadline for submitting my message in writing so that the simultaneous translators at the Conference could familiarize themselves ahead of time.

The Lord came through for me. I felt the leading and the inspiration of the Holy Spirit as I prayerfully prepared.

On arriving in Amsterdam I found that there

was a strong contingency of leaders from the Caribbean, most of them known to me because of our various endeavors in the kingdom of God across the region. They assured me of their prayer and support for my assignment.

The time came. I stood in the pulpit at Amsterdam looking in the faces of that vast company and in the faces of leaders eminently more qualified than myself and remembered the scripture from Jeremiah 1:8-10 that says:

"Do not be afraid of their faces, for I am with you to deliver you. Behold, I have put My words in your mouth."

Unlike most of the presenters who read their presentations, I preached. I felt the anointing of the Lord carrying me along. The Lord blessed and the audience became responsive to the Word! I discharged what the Lord had given me and felt His approval as I stepped off the platform.

"Come and listen you that fear the Lord and let me tell you what He has done for me!" For me! Yes, me…addressing a conference like this?? I knew what David felt like as he stood before the giant Goliath. I knew what the little boy in John 6:8 must have felt when he saw how Jesus used the little that he had to feed 5000! Like David

and that little boy I can't help but invite folks to, "Come and listen and let me tell you what the Lord has done!"

Many years have passed since that event but I am still praising the Lord for His divine enabling in the preparation, the delivery and the reception of that message. Without a doubt one of the greatest experiences in my preaching career. You will find the entire message included as an appendix at the end of this book.

Broken

I thank the Lord upon every memory of my
mother-in-law, Mrs. Marjorie Elaine Wright. We
had a beautiful mother-in-law/son-in-law
relationship. In fact she had three children of
her own (my wife Sonia and two sons, Raymond
and Howard) but she made me feel like I was
her favorite child. (I had a great and wonderful
relationship also with my father-in-law-Franklin
Wright, but this story is about my mother-in-
law).

In August 2005 my mother-in-law turned over
$5034 to me to be used for her burial. I gave her
a written statement guaranteeing that at least
that same sum would be available towards her
burial expenses. In 2006 I proceeded to invest it
in a Jamaican Christian organization trading in
foreign exchange which promised monthly
interest rates beyond any other investment at the
time. The investment did very well for a two
year period – impressive enough for me to move
all of my little retirement savings into that
foreign-exchange portfolio to improve provision
for old age for Sonia and me.

Unfortunately, the investment collapsed in 2008

sending shock waves into the lives of Sonia and me, -and many others. This investment collapse was the Jamaican equivalent of the Bernie Madoff Ponzi fiasco of that same year. We lost all of our savings. Everything, including the money to bury my mother-in-law.

My mother-in-law died in March 2009. It was my responsibility to cover the expenses of her burial – but now I have no money – had lost it all – I was broke!

Nonetheless she had to be buried. In desperation I cried to the Lord for His help.

With great embarrassment I opened my heart to my pastor and dear friend, Rev. Hervin Green, Pastor of Metropolitan Baptist Church. He was very empathetic. We agreed on the date for the funeral service to be held in the Metropolitan Baptist Chapel. I left from there to go talk to the undertakers, praying all the way for the Lord's favor.

I knew the undertaker personally having done several funerals with them during my years as pastor of Metropolitan Baptist Church. With great embarrassment I shared with him that I wanted his funeral home to handle the burial of my mother-in-law. I explained to him that she had given me money to cover her funeral but that the money for her funeral and all of my life's savings been lost in the collapse of the foreign currency investment program in Jamaica I told him I was broke – I had no money to cover his services – but she needed to be buried. I asked him, "What can you do for me under these circumstances?" He said to me, "Your mother-in-law will be buried, pastor. Let me see what I can do." With that he took a moment and worked on some calculations, and then he said to me, "Pastor, I am going to do something special for you. For the preparation of the body, the casket, the limousine service and the gravesite, we will do it for $6500." I was expecting a much bigger figure. I jumped up, grabbed his hand and said, yes! I agree to that! Thank you!"

He then said he would give me three months in which to pay up the $6500. I agreed and we shook hands once again. He then gave me the burial contract to sign, but the contract said that I had already paid the $6500 (which is their standard procedure to be paid in advance). I protested – I told him I could not sign it because I had not paid any money. I would be guilty of making a false statement. He insisted that I sign the document. "I am the owner. I have a gentleman's agreement with you. I trust you. Sign the document as I do not want anyone in the office to know of our special agreement – it will come back to haunt me. Please sign the contract Pastor Gallimore." I felt exonerated and I signed the document, thanking him profusely.

The Lord had come through for me once again. Praise His name!

I came home rejoicing and shared it with my wife. My mother-in-law would be buried in style. Needless to say we prayed daily for the Lord's provision to meet the three month deadline.

In the course of the week cards of sympathy came from various family members and friends, many of whom enclosed a gift to help with her funeral expenses. So much so that on the day of the funeral I was able to hand the undertaker a check for $3000. *To God be the glory!*

The afternoon of the funeral I sat down at home with my wife and her two brothers and we reminisced about their mother's life, about how the funeral service had gone, and I shared with my brothers-in-law the financial challenges, the special arrangement with the undertakers, how God had graciously provided so that I was able to pay the undertakers $3000 that morning, and was now facing into the remaining $3500 to be paid off in just under three months time.

While we were having this conversation the phone rang. Pastor Green was on the phone. He invited me to come to see him up at the church office. I immediately went to the church office. Pastor Green said to me, "Brother Gerry, I think you know that you are well loved in this church. Your brothers and sisters here want to share in the funeral expenses with you." And with that he handed me an envelope with a check for $3500! I was overcome. With tears running down my face I thanked him profusely as I told him what had transpired with the undertaker. Together we rejoiced at the Lord's faithfulness and gave the Lord thanks for His miraculous provision.

The following Monday morning I went down to the undertaker and paid him the outstanding balance of $3500. In the words of the Psalmist David, I am shouting for all who will listen…

"Come and listen you that fear the Lord and let me tell you what He has done for me!"

YES—Yes…*"The Lord has done great things for me whereof I am glad!"*

(N.B. So as not to compromise the funeral home or the kind owner I have refrained from revealing the names.)

Beautiful!

While in Jamaica on a preaching mission in 2012 my dear friend and esteemed Christian brother, businessman, Robert Levy, invited me to have breakfast at his home. As we chatted together I happened to mention that Sonia and I would be celebrating our 50th wedding anniversary in 2013. Robbie wanted to know how we were going to celebrate our anniversary. I responded that we had no plans; we would just wait to see what if anything the Lord may do. Robert immediately offered to provide us with a family vacation to a resort on the south coast of Jamaica! I was taken aback. This was totally unexpected. I immediately accepted. The details of the dates to be finalized. There would be space for our entire family – children and grandchildren.

Understandably, there was great elation in my family when I shared this with them.

On July 6, 2013, 14 of us in the family spent a fabulous vacation at this seaside resort – all accommodation, meals and amenities provided at no cost to us – all covered by my beloved Christian brother! A bill that would have run into multiplied thousands of $$!!!

"Come and listen you that fear the Lord and let me tell you what He has done for me!"

*"The Lord…*Yes, THE LORD *has done great things for me whereof I am truly glad!"*

Bountiful

Donovan and I have been friends for many years. We hail from the same island of Jamaica. We have gone to several world conferences together. I have gone and ministered at his church in the middle of the USA and he has ministered at the church I pastored in Florida. Donovan is a visionary with a ministry to the leadership of African-American churches in the USA. We keep in touch with each other sharing updates on our families, our ministries and our mutual friends. Like me he has faced financial challenges in his personal life and in his ministry.

He called me in July 2018 to share with me some developments in his life and in the life of his children. He had lost his wife of many years only a few weeks earlier. I was delighted to hear how he was being sustained by the grace of the Lord. He very proudly shared with me about the Lord's call on the life of his son, a successful architect, to move to the Dominican Republic to do ministry. As a dad his heart was overflowing with joy and pride. Also he shared with me the special working of the Holy Spirit in the life of his son. And then he went on to share with me of God's miraculous provision in his life enabling him to pay off all his financial debts. We rejoiced together for the Lord's goodness. Then he said to me (knowing that Sonia and I live by faith), "How are things with you Gerry?" I demurred for a moment and not wanting the Lord to be upset with me, I answered, "Challenging, my brother." At that very moment my wife Sonia was on 'all fours' (crawling on hands and feet) going up the steps to our bedroom on the second floor. I continued to Donovan, "At this moment as I speak to you it pains me to see Sonia on all fours making her way up to our bedroom on the second floor." He said to me, "Gerry you need to install a stair lift." I agreed with him. I told him my research indicated that a new stair-lift would cost about $5000 and a used one around $2500, "but that kind of money is beyond us right now." He and I chatted some more and as we closed our phone call he said to me, "Gerry, I am going to send you something." I said, "bless you my brother" and hung up.

I shared the conversation with Sonia and she said to me, "So how much do you think he might send us?" I said to her, "I have no idea – maybe $100, maybe $200 – whatever he sends we will give God thanks."

A few minutes later my phone rang and there

was someone on the line from Acorn Stairlifts saying, "We understand that you are in need of a stair lift."

I am not proud of my reaction. It was one of annoyance. I thought to myself how could Donovan do this to me? Informing a salesman at Acorn Stairlift so he can harass me about a purchase. I stopped the salesman short and told him in no uncertain terms, "Yes, I am in need of a stair lift, but I have no ability to purchase one so let us not waste time with this call."

I was getting ready to hang up when he said, "But Sir, the gentleman said he would pay for it!" I was flabbergasted. Speechless. Embarrassed. Deeply reprimanded in my spirit by the Holy Spirit for my sorry attitude and my statements of annoyance.

"What did you just say?" I asked the salesman not quite trusting my ears. He repeated, "The gentleman said he will cover the cost." My attitude changed immediately. I apologized to the salesman and asked for his forgiveness. We agreed on a date for his representative to come to our house and take the necessary measurements.

The representative came, took the measurements and called my friend Donovan to advise him it would cost $4000 and that they needed the payment upfront. I waited in silence as they spoke not believing that Donovan would be able to cover that kind of cost. But he agreed. One week later a brand new Acorn Stairlift was installed at our house and my wife Sonia now goes up and down the stairs in dignity, often times carrying loads of dirty or clean clothes or whatever. My brothers and sisters, surely you understand when I say with a Psalmist...

"Come and listen you that fear the Lord and let me tell you what He has done for me!"

YES—Yes..."*The Lord has done great things for me whereof I am glad!"* I am not just 'glad'... I am 'shouting-out-loud' glad!

Bulwark

I must begin this chapter by quoting Isaiah 43:1-3. It says,

"But now, thus says the Lord who created you, and He who formed you: 'Fear not, for I have redeemed you; I have called you by your name; you are Mine. When you pass through the waters, I will be with you: and through the rivers, they shall not overflow you. When you walk through the fire, you shall not be burned, nor shall the flame scorch you. For I am the Lord your God, The Holy One of Israel, your Savior."

These are great words for the believer to stand on in times of trouble. Great words that allay fears and minister peace as we pass through the waters and through the rivers and through the fires.

I invite you to walk with me through one of the most difficult periods in the life of Sonia and me.

Let me be the first one to tell you, I am no superhero. In my humanity I am afflicted with the same every day anxieties and concerns that afflict the rest of us, **_but_** I am redeemed by what the Psalmist David says in Psalm 103:14, *"The Lord knows my frame; He remembers that I am dust."* He <u>knows</u> my frame and He remembers that I am dust! Praise His Name! Further, He comes alongside me reminding me of His promise in Isaiah 43:1-3 (quoted above). If you are familiar with the poem **_"Footprints"_,** my story below is one of those times when there was only one set of footprints... **_His_**!

I am married to a remarkable woman! I met her in July 1961. She was part of a sold-out group of young people who were holding an open-air evangelistic meeting on King Street (the busiest street of the city of Kingston) on a Saturday afternoon (the busiest day at the busiest hour). As I passed by she handed me a tract and I was attracted! She was beautiful. She was on fire for Jesus (as mentioned in chapter one, a great story for another time!). We got married on February 23, 1963 – 57 years ago, and as they say, the rest is history. She is an honors graduate of the University of the West Indies in Social Work. She has been twice nationally honored by the Government of Jamaica. Firstly with the Badge of Honor for Meritorious Work in the field of Social Work; and the prestigious Order of Distinction (OD) for her contribution to Jamaican national life.

We relocated from Jamaica to Florida in 1989 to facilitate my work as Area Director for YFCI/Americas. My wife Sonia did graduate work at St. Thomas University qualifying as a Marriage and Family Life Therapist. She has practiced in this field for nearly 3 decades as a licensed therapist.

After serving six years as President/CEO of Youth For Christ International, I stepped down from that role and was named YFCI International Ambassador. Sonia and I relocated from Singapore in 1996 to our home in Pembroke Pines, Florida. From my base in Florida my role was to serve YFCI at the behest of the new President/CEO.

With permission of the new President/CEO, I became Pastor of Metropolitan Baptist Church in Hollywood, Florida in 1997.

Sonia worked on a part-time basis as an adjunct therapist with an agency in Miami doing group therapy with a group of the agency's clients as requested from time to time by the agency. On turning up at the agency one morning in September 2011 she found the agency under siege by the FBI, with all the agency staff arrested! She was prevented from entering the compound.

In April of 2013, 1 year and 7 months later, three FBI officers turned up at our house informing Sonia that the agency was involved in Medicare fraud and proceeded to interrogate Sonia, accusing her of complicity in this fraud, in that her group session reports were part and parcel of fraudulent claims made by the agency. She explained her role – that she was 'on-call' staff responding to ad hoc requests from the agency to do group counseling. She submitted written reports on each counseling session to the agency administration, but had no knowledge of how or what the reports were used for, apart from client record keeping.

Needless to say this visit and interrogation by the FBI was very upsetting. The tenor of this interrogation indicated an intention to indict.

We immediately notified our children – Trudy, Oliver and Lisa, as well as Debbie and Mark, two of our adopted children living nearby. They advised securing legal representation and Debbie recommended the name of a prominent Miami lawyer.

Prosecution by the FBI is a serious matter!

We committed the matter to the Lord and made an appointment to see the lawyer. Adopted son Mark (himself a lawyer) drove us down to see this Miami lawyer. The lawyer's office was decorated with many citations.

The lawyer, a well-dressed, personable man, exuded a competent calming confidence as we shared the situation with him. He indicated that the case would be a complicated one, very likely lasting several weeks before a judge. He would take the case but his fee would be $100,000 and we would need to bring in a down payment of $25,000 within seven days. I was blown away! I had never before had reason to engage the services of a lawyer and had absolutely no idea of this kind of fee.

I immediately shared with the lawyer that we were retired missionaries living by faith, and while we would be happy to have him represent us, we had no way of meeting those terms. Mark asked him what was the best that he could do and after a few moments of reflection he said that given what I had shared he would reduce his fee to $80,000 but needed to have the $25,000 within seven days to indicate that we were serious to engage his services.

I was about to protest the seven day timetable for the $25,000, but Mark stopped me and advised the lawyer that we accepted his terms. With a very anxious heart overwhelmed with what had just transpired, I said to the lawyer, "I hope you don't mind but I would like for us to close with a word of prayer asking God's blessing. He joined hands with us as we bowed and prayed in his office. I did not know it then but found out on our next visit that the lawyer is a committed Christian!

When we stepped out of his office walking towards the car I said to Mark that he surprised me by accepting the lawyer's terms. Where will we find $80,000 and where will we come up with $25,000 within 7 days?? Mark said he felt confident that we had the right lawyer and that we just had to pray and trust the Lord to provide the funds.

It was for me a very tall order! One of the biggest challenges to our faith. You can understand that we were frightened and cried to the Lord for His help. I immediately called my brother Rupert in Jamaica and shared this development with him for urgent prayer.

The year 2013 was our 50th wedding anniversary (as mentioned in an earlier chapter). Our very dear friend and Christian brother Robert Levy had very kindly offered Sonia and me a one week holiday at an exquisite Jamaican south coast resort as our wedding anniversary present!!

Two days after the above meeting with the lawyer, we arrived in Jamaica for the wedding anniversary holiday.

My brother Rupert drove me back from the south coast into Kingston for a breakfast appointment he had set up with about 12 Christian brothers for me to share with them with what happened and the challenge of raising $25,000 by the following Monday. I opened my heart to them. They prayed with me and then Tony Williamson challenged each person to make a commitment towards this need – to be honored there and then, or in time for me to take it with me when returning to the USA that weekend.

US$14,000 were contributed at that breakfast!!
Praise the name of the Lord!!

I was blown away by this response. My faith in the Lord's provision was greatly strengthened. When we got back to Florida we found promises from several of my brothers and sisters living in the USA and in Canada, providing the other $11,000!!

On July 15, 2013, the 'within seven days' deadline set by the lawyer, we paid him by certified check the sum of $25,000!

*"Come and listen you that fear the Lord and let me
tell you what He has done for me!"* YES—
Yes…*"The Lord has done great things for us whereof
I am glad!"*

Sonia was totally innocent of any wrongdoing.
There was indeed malpractice at the agency
where she worked on a "on call" basis. But she
knew nothing of the malpractice, nor the fact
that the agency was padding her reports (among
others), to make false claims against Medicare.
Fortunately, she had kept all of her diaries and
had all of her reports in her computer. She
printed off box loads of these reports for the
lawyer.

October 2, 2014 is a never to be forgotten day!
We were awakened at about 5:30am that
morning to the sound of loud rapping on our
front door. Sonia went down the stairs ahead of
me to check. I followed closely behind to see the
front door opened, five or six heavily armed FBI
agents in our living room and some 8 police cars
with flashing lights outside our door. They
ordered me to come downstairs.

"What's going on? What's going on? Where is
Sonia?" I asked in panic.

They had arrested Sonia!

She was standing outside the door in her pajamas. Her hands behind her back. Handcuffed!

An FBI officer informed me – "Your wife has been arrested for Medicare fraud." I was terrified! Frightened! This can't be happening. Not to Sonia and Gerry Gallimore. We are God's servants.

Suddenly, I felt I was going to collapse. One of the female FBI agents helped me to a seat. I was ordered not to move. The agent informed me they were going to take Sonia away for processing.

In her pajamas.

I objected strongly. "She needs to put on some clothes. You cannot take her away like that. Please allow her to dress." They yielded – but wanted to know if there was anyone else in the house. The female FBI agent accompanied Sonia to our bedroom so she could change.

They took her away in handcuffs. One of the lowest moments in my life.

The female FBI agent wrote down the address of the Federal Court before which Sonia would be arraigned later that morning.

I called our three children immediately. They were devastated. Devastated for their mom as well as for me. I called adopted son Mark who immediately offered to drive me to the court. I called my pastor, Rev. Hervin Green and shared with him. He kindly offered to accompany me to the court.

Five of us – Pastor Green, Bro. Ivan (Chairman of Deacons at our church), Mark, son Oliver and I met at our home for prayer before leaving for court that morning.

Sonia and two other persons from the agency were indicted under the same charge that morning. On the first of the three persons accused the court set a bail bond of $750,000! I froze. If the court set the same bail bond for Sonia... it could not be met. The thought of her having to spend even one night in a lockup was more than I could bear. In desperation I cried to the Lord. The others with me were doing the same thing.

Sonia's name was called, the indictment read and her 'not guilty' plea entered. Her lawyer stood to his feet and addressed the judge informing the court of Sonia's age, of her missionary service, of her character within society, that she had no prior indictment and was not a flight risk. The judge cut him short, reminding him that this was not a trial and asking what was his point. Her lawyer asked the court that Sonia be released on her own recognizance without bail. The judge turned to the prosecutor and asked him what was his demand. I could hardly believe my ears when I heard the prosecutor say that he had no objection. Sonia was released without a bail bond!

"Come and listen you that fear the Lord and let me tell you what He has done for me!" YES— Yes…*"The Lord has done great things for us whereof we are glad!"*

I will not take the time to give you all the many other details of this three year ordeal – this three year trial of our faith – and yes, triumph of our faith. Because of the enormous amount of evidential material to wade through and the projection that the actual trial would take weeks before the court, the lawyer twice increased his charges. Each time the Lord came through for us. Members of our family and members of the Christian community stood in sacrificial solidarity with us for the means as well as the outcome of this case.

In June of 2016, 3+ years later, in the Lord's miraculous intervention all charges in the case against Sonia were dropped! As the prosecutor said in a brief pretrial consultation just before the wrapping up of the case, "We are satisfied, Mrs. Gallimore, that you are not a criminal. You happened to work for a bad agency." When the court convened moments after this, the charges were dropped and the nightmare was over, and Sonia's name was cleared!

The Lord gave us a Christian lawyer who did an outstanding job of representation. Through family, friends, churches and the Christian community, the lawyer's fee of $154,000 was provided!! And there was no court trial!!!

You will forgive me for shouting hallelujah! Praise the Lord! Thank you Jesus! You will understand when like David in Psalm 66:16 I keep on saying:

"Come and listen you that fear the Lord and let me tell you what He has done for me!"

YES—Yes..."*The Lord has done great things for us whereof we are glad!"*

This nightmare of over three years came to an end in answer to the prayers of God's people and the promise of God's Word. We remain forever grateful to our blessed Lord and Savior Jesus Christ, and to all who supported us with prayer, encouragement, and financial help with the legal expenses. To our attorney, Dr. Larry Handfield, we remain very grateful indeed for his effective representation.

Basis

I have quoted Psalm 66:16 numerous times as I
have rejoiced again and again in sharing with
you some of what the Lord has done for me.
This verse gives me a Biblical basis for sharing as
I follow the Psalmist's example as he invites
others to join him in celebrating God's
underserved goodness in his life.

As you know David is the author of most of the
Psalms, but not all of them. Other servants of
God like Asaph, the sons of Korah, Solomon,
Moses, Ethan (and perhaps Ezra) also wrote
Psalms. We do not know for sure who is the
author of Psalm 66, but there is no reason to
doubt that it is David, for it is 'Davidic in its
style and has nothing unsuited to his times.' In
the absence of evidence to the contrary, I am one
of many who believe that this Psalm was penned
by David.

My brothers and sisters, genuine Christianity
involves at least two things.
- An *inward experience* of God's grace, and
- Some *outward expression and evidence* of
  that grace at work in our lives.

In other words, genuine Christianity involves an inward experience of the saving grace of Jesus Christ in a person's life, which in turn must produce some convincing outward evidence that there has been an inward experience of salvation. Any one of these without the other, calls into question the genuineness of one's religious experience! If we claim to be saved – to be Christians – but there is no change in our lifestyle or behavior, clearly something is wrong. If we are doing good works and good deeds but cannot testify to a salvation experience with the Lord Jesus Christ...something of vital import is missing.

These two things are necessary and the Psalmist had both. The Psalmist here is not a cold believer with Sunday morning religion only. No! He knew God for himself. This God had captured his heart and he was not ashamed or hesitant to give vibrant expression to his faith. Hear him in verse 1:

"Make a joyful shout to God, all the earth! Sing out the honor of His name; make His praise glorious."
He seems to think that keeping quiet about what God has done is bad for one's health! Hear him in Psalm 32:3

"When I kept silent my bones grow old."

So he issues this invitation in Psalm 66:16 ***"Come and listen you that fear the Lord and let me tell*** *you what He has done for me!"* As I said earlier there is something on his heart bubbling over and he can't keep quiet about it. He has to tell somebody. So he issues the invitation for folks to gather around him, "Come" he says, "Come and listen, I have got something to tell you."

WHY DOES THE PSALMIST THINK IT IS IMPORTANT TO SPEAK ABOUT WHAT GOD HAS DONE FOR HIM?

HOW CAN <u>WE</u> JUSTIFY THESE KINDS OF TESTIMONIES?

Firstly, **A REASON CONNECTED WITH GOD**:

These stories are an expression of gratitude to God. It is an expression of our gratitude to Him – our desire to honor and bring glory to Him. How base it is to hide what God has done—to fail to give God credit for what He has done – to thank Him publicly for His benevolence and His kindly intervention on our behalf.

Must Jesus say again, *"Were there not 10 cleansed, but where are the nine?" (Luke 17:17)*
CLEANSED--but no thanks for the precious blood?
HEALED--but no praise for the Healer?

SAVED-- but no praise for the One who paid the supreme price to rescue us?

BLESSED--but no recognition, no thanks, no gratitude to our Blessed Lord?

It would be base indeed! There is a reason connected with God, to give Him thanks, to give Him praise, to bring glory to His name for what He has done for us!

How can we justify these kinds of testimonies? Firstly, **A REASON CONNECTED WITH GOD:**

Secondly, **A REASON CONNECTED WITH OURSELVES**:

<u>It is good for our souls</u>. It keeps alive in our hearts God's marvelous grace and doings-- lest we forget!! For sometimes under the stress of the moment, when the economy is down, when the pressure is on, and when problems arise...that is when we must remind ourselves of what God has done for us LEST WE FORGET! As the songwriter says there are times:
 "When you look at others with their lands and gold,
 Think that Christ has promised you His wealth untold,
 Count your many blessings; name them one by one,

and it will remind you what the Lord has done"

How can we justify these kinds of testimonies?
Firstly, A REASON CONNECTED WITH GOD:

Secondly, A REASON CONNECTED WITH
OURSELVES:

Thirdly, **A REASON CONNECTED WITH
OTHERS--THOSE WE ADDRESS!**

These testimonials may be the means that God
uses for their salvation, as they hear us testify
about where God has brought us from, and the
changes He has made in our lives through the
work of His Son on the cross. There are few
things so powerful as a man or a woman sharing
with others the story of how Jesus saved them.
Yes, *"Come and let me tell you what He has done for
my soul."*

Our testimony to others of what God has
done for us serves to encourage others and to
build up their faith in God's ability and His
willingness to do the same for them.
Which of us is not indebted to the stories of
Abraham, Moses, David, Peter, Paul, George
Mueller, David Livingstone, Billy Graham and
so many others? Their testimonies have done a
lot to call us to repentance, to build up our faith
in God, and to ground our faith in Him.

My brothers and sisters, how can we justify these kinds of testimonies?
– A REASON CONNECTED WITH GOD.
– A REASON CONNECTED WITH OURSELVES.
– A REASON CONNECTED WITH OTHERS.
And **A REASON CONNECTED WITH THE FAITH**.

Hear me, my brothers and sisters, our faith is not some stale creed, nor sterile philosophy of a long dead Prophet. *NO! OUR GOD IS NOT DEAD! CHRIST JESUS OUR SAVIOR IS ALIVE!!*

Folks need to know that <u>our faith is the dynamic involvement with a God who is still active in the lives of His children!</u> Christianity is about the mighty miracle working God who delights to break into men's lives with salvation, guidance and power. We should not have to reach back into antiquity only for evidence of our God's working power, but we ought to be able to say to folks in the here and now *"Come and listen and let me tell you what God has done for me!"*

Men and women need to know that Christianity is not only about mighty profound transcendent concepts to engage the mind, and about which men write massive theological volumes. Yes, it is this – for the truth of the faith transcends all other academic disciplines. But it is more than that--it is also about <u>current experiences</u>, <u>current happenings</u>, <u>current relationships</u> between that God and His creatures. The God of Christianity delights to come down to where we are and touch our lives and circumstances with His Almighty power and redeeming grace.

He is real!
He knows me and hears my cry!
He does things in me and for me and with me--
so that I cannot help but say with Psalmist,
"Come and listen, you who fear God, and let me tell you what He has done for me!"

Oh, praise His name – this God, my God waits to do something for somebody reading this report. Is it you? Is it you?? He waits to touch somebody, to save somebody, to fix somebody, to bless somebody. Is it you? Is it you?
Call on Him right now – let Him meet your need so you too can say like the psalmist, *"Come and listen all you who fear God and let me tell you what he has done for me."*
        Amen!

My brothers and sisters,
"The Lord has done – <u>and continues to do</u> – great things for <u>me</u> whereof I am glad."   -
Gerry Gallimore

Appendix 1 Amsterdam 2000

Conference of Preaching Evangelists

Participants - Amsterdam 2000

Another view of Amsterdam 2000 plenary session

Plenary Message by Dr. Gerry Gallimore
at Amsterdam 2000 Conference of Preaching
Evangelists; July 29-August 6, 2000

"THE EVANGELIST COMMUNICATES EFFECTIVELY"

"Do the work of an evangelist!" 2 Tim. 4:5

Esteemed elders in the faith, brothers and sisters,
ladies and gentlemen, I am indeed grateful to
God, to His servant Dr. Graham and to the
Amsterdam 2000 Planning Committee for the
high honor accorded me to address you today
on this subject which epitomizes what we as
evangelists hope to do whenever God gives us
the opportunity to share the good news of the
Gospel.

Please turn with me to 2 Timothy 4:1-5.

The Apostle Paul here lays upon us the
seriousness of our responsibility and the
awesomeness of our evangelistic task. Ours is
the grand privilege and urgent responsibility:
– To preach the Word;
– To announce to lost, rebellious humanity the
only message that saves;
- To be a vital part of preparing the world for the

imminent return of the One who will judge the living and the dead.

- We must preach the Word, in season and out of season for Paul's prophecy recorded here has come to pass in our time. The time of unsound doctrine and reverse values is not out there in some distant far off future. It is now! People are turning from the truth and are embracing myths. Even as we meet here this morning, the devil has an army of influencers on the airwaves, in the classrooms, in the print media, on the Internet, in the cinemas and elsewhere, promoting unbiblical falsehood. Against this background our Lord and Savior this morning lays upon those of us in this room the same compelling, authoritative marching orders He gave to the eleven evangelists just before He left for glory, "All authority in Heaven and in earth is mine, He says, 'therefore go, go! go! into all the world and preach the Gospel." (Matt. 28:18; Mk.16:15) He sends us today, as He sent them back then, to counter the deception and the falsehood by telling men the good news of the Gospel, the liberating truth that ...

–the power of sin and addiction is broken,

–the promoter of sin and rebellion is defeated,

–the way to heaven and to peace with God is open,

– salvation full and free is available to all and that ...

the grave is no longer a dead-end street, but

hallelujah, it has become a thoroughfare!!

This is our message. This is the awesome, exciting, life transforming, soul saving truth we must convey to this post-modern, fat-free, cholesterol removed, cyber-surfing, spiritually lost world.

And if the eleven did it back then, so can we! Without radio, or television, or PA systems, or motor cars, or airplanes, or any of the fancy gadgets available to us ... they faithfully and effectively evangelized their world. So can we ... so must we! And this morning from the balcony of heaven they cheer us on, "Preach the Word!" they shout. "Do the work of an evangelist ... make full proof of your ministry ... be ready at all times, in season and out of season ... for the time is short." (2Tim 4:1-2; 1 Cor.7:29)

My brothers and sisters, if you and I are going to be effective in evangelizing this generation ...
1. **THERE IS A BIBLICAL MESSAGE WE MUST PROCLAIM...**

It is the same Biblical message proclaimed by those evangelists of that first century! The message of the atoning, redemptive, substitutionary, once-and-for-all work of God's Son, Jesus Christ on the cross of Calvary 2000 years ago. Brothers and sisters, we have no liberty in the 21st century to alter this message, to water it down, or to substitute any aspect of it with something more palatable to modern man. Our job is to proclaim it under the power of the Holy Spirit. We can preach no other Gospel, lest the curse of Galatians 1:7 fall on us. Our message must be "according to the Scriptures;" that Gospel "which was once and for all delivered to the saints."

If we are going to discharge our Lord's command and fulfill Paul's charge to 'make full proof of our evangelistic ministry' we must get to know the message well, so that we can proclaim the message clearly. Like with any other subject, competence is vital for effectiveness and for credibility. Those early evangelists spent three years of intense training under the tutelage of the Master Himself. They watched Him at work. They went on mission with Him. They were corrected by Him. They followed Him to the Cross. They experienced the resurrection and the empowering by the Holy Spirit. We must not be deceived into thinking that we can be effective in our age without equal qualifications, without spending time with the Master, and time in His Word. For it is the Word that reveals that mankind outside of Christ is lost in sin, groping in darkness, living in estrangement from God (Psalm 51:5; Isaiah 53:6; Romans 3:23).

Modern man has made enormous achievements. That we cannot deny. But we must not be deceived or intimidated by the pretences of these achievements. We must know assuredly that technology cannot save him; neither can science nor education or politics, nor can Wall Street buy him peace with God.

We must preach the lostness of man for this is Biblical. But more, we must preach that in his lostness mankind faces grave peril, for this too is Biblical. But thanks be to God, that's not all we must preach for the message of the Bible is Good News ... great good news for lost mankind facing grave peril. There is hope, blessed life-transforming, peril averting, destiny changing, soul saving hope in Jesus Christ. However, we must not fail to declare that **THIS HOPE IS IN JESUS CHRIST, AND IN HIM ALONE!** Jesus is not 'a way' among other ways. No! He is **'THE WAY'** --the only way! Despite how narrow and unpopular this concept is to modern man we cannot equivocate. Like Peter in Acts 4:12 we must urgently, lovingly yet uncompromisingly tell lost men and women that "there is no other name under heaven, given to men by which we must be saved" except the name of Jesus. My brothers and sisters, if you and I as evangelists are going to be effective in reaching this generation for Christ and His kingdom, this is the Biblical message we must proclaim.

But equally important...
- **THERE IS A BIBLICAL INTEGRITY WE MUST POSSESS.**

If we are going to be effective evangelists, the message must be right, but equally important the messenger must be righteous! Our words must be backed by our deeds. There must be harmony between the message we preach and the lives we live. The incarnation of Jesus Christ tells us that the Word must be fleshed out. It is with shame we must admit that a major crisis facing the church today is a crisis of integrity! The voice of the Apostle Paul pleads with us from the pages of Scripture, "I beseech you, walk worthy of the Name, walk worthy of the calling" (Eph. 4:1). The Apostle Peter solemnly exhorts us, "Be holy for He is holy" (1 Pet. 1:16). Our lives must line up with the written Word and with the message we proclaim. Integrity, purity, transparency must be the possession and the character of all who preach the Gospel.
So we must "discipline our bodies and bring them into subjection, lest when we have preached to others, we ourselves become disqualified, become castaways" (1 Cor. 9:27). God forbid that this should be heaven's verdict on any of us here today.

Basic to this Biblical integrity is the requirement that we must be converted to Christ (John 3:3, 6-

7). I trust I have not embarrassed anyone here with this simplistic, but oh so paramount statement! As evangelists we must be able to testify to a personal life-changing encounter with Jesus Christ. No course in theology or homiletics, however prestigious the institution, can replace this basic need. No ordination, however elaborate, will suffice. If by any chance at a great conference like this, there is someone, maybe an ordained preacher like John Wesley was, but as you sit here this morning you are conscious of something missing in your spiritual life, may I plead with you, don't leave this conference without stepping into this vital relationship with the Savior. Biblical integrity requires preachers not only to be persons with personal experience of conversion, but also that we must be committed to Christ and the cause of evangelism as a current, active, present reality in our lives.

Evangelism never travels in neutral gear or on an empty tank. The dynamism of evangelism is always in forward gear and under the fullness of the Spirit's power. For that to happen there must be genuine commitment to the Lord and to the cause for which He died. This commitment is not optional for any Christian and for those of us called to the office of the Evangelist it is an indispensable imperative. We evangelize or fossilize. We preach or we perish.

The Biblical integrity we must possess requires not only that we must be converted to Christ and that we must be committed to His Cause, but also that our evangelism must be constrained by His love.

Wouldn't it be great if, like Paul, all of us here could say with equal sincerity that it is the love of Christ which 'constrains' our evangelism. That self-sacrificing love displayed at the cross for lost mankind, that this is what constrains us. Above all other motivations this is what compels us, moves us, energizes us. Is this true of us? Is this our prime motivation or has something less worthy captured our hearts? Vain glory, perhaps? Infatuation with ourselves? Loving the spotlight and the public attention?? My brothers and sisters, is it money? Fame? Glory? In the final analysis, are we servants or showmen? Can we say with Isaac Watts:

"When I survey the wondrous Cross,
On which the Prince of Glory died,
My richest gain I count but loss,
And pour contempt on all my pride.

Were the whole realm of nature mine,
That were a present far too small,
Love so amazing, so divine,
Demands my soul, my life, my all."

No other motive is worthy of Him. The love of Christ ... let it constrain you! Let it consume you!

If we would be evangelists communicating effectively...
- **THERE IS A BIBLICAL MESSAGE WE MUST PROCLAIM**
- **THERE IS A BIBLICAL INTEGRITY WE MUST POSSESS, but also ...**
- **THERE IS A BIBLICAL STRATEGY WE MUST PURSUE**

It is very important to be orthodox in our message. It is very important to be authentic in our integrity. But as evangelists we can still fail in our mission, if the message we send is not received and understood by our hearers. Then we would have merely occupied time, merely put some words in the wind. We would have failed for we would not have communicated. For communication is more than mere transmission, it is more than mere proclamation. This is the heart of our subject for this morning. You and I have an inescapable responsibility to ensure as much as it lies within our power to do so, that the message we send is understood in the way we intended. That people don't only hear words, but that the truth of the Gospel is packaged and delivered in terms understandable to their ears, so we can reach their minds and their hearts. The evangelist communicates when the message delivered, is understood in the way the evangelist intended. The evangelist communicates effectively, when the message delivered is understood clearly enough to be used of God to bring conviction to the hearer's heart.

Where can we turn to learn the rudiments of this important skill? May I suggest that we already have a textbook on communication in our hands? The Bible, studied under the guidance of the Holy Spirit, can become to us the greatest textbook on the effective communication of the Gospel. Go to the pages of the Gospels; watch the Master communicator Himself, our Lord Jesus Christ at work. Go to the Book of Acts and to the epistles and observe the early evangelists in their work and in their writings and you and I will learn the strategy we must pursue to be effective communicators in this and any age. We will learn that we must be **CREATIVE IN OUR APPROACH**.

Creativity is demanded in every age and most certainly in this fast paced, rapidly changing world in which we live. A world where change takes place with the speed and turbulence of a ride down a white water river. We are swamped by the sheer volume of it all. New technology rolls off the assembly line only to become obsolete by the time it hits the marketplace.

This is our world. Information and ideas move at cyberspeed across cyberspace. If we are going to be on mission for God and make an impact on this kind of world, then more of us will have to change our old resistant mindset and catch up with reality. This is tough, for some of us missed the train into the 20th century. But try as we may we can never move the world back to the cart and buggy days. We are in a new century filled with the same age old problems that Paul and Peter faced, but complicated with such things as computers, condoms, same sex marriages, satellites, television, New Age religions, cybercrime, and the Internet where sleaze and pornography are only a 'click' away.

To minister effectively to this age we must become creative in our communication!
We must become flexible. Principles do not change, but strategies must. Like Paul in 1 Corinthians 9:22, "To the weak we must become weak, to win the weak. We must become all things to all men so that by all possible means we may save some." The motor vehicle gear that takes us effectively over the plain will not take us over the hill. The clothes for summer will not do for winter. Neither will a 'one-size-fits-all' mentality do. There is a cultural Tower of Babel out there demanding of us creativity.
Traditional, mediocre, cookie cutter approach to evangelism will suffocate in the highly

competitive, rapidly changing inter-active culture of the 21st century.

We need Spirit-led, God honoring creativity to enhance our effectiveness. I submit that the new technology, the praise and worship music, the new translations of Scripture are not demons to be resisted, brothers, and sisters. They are gifts from the Creator and His Spirit to be embraced and to be creatively used. The evangelist who is creative in approach enhances the chances for a hearing and for effectiveness.

Secondly, we must be **CONTEXTUAL IN OUR APPLICATION** ... because meaning always occurs in context. The context determines to a great extent the meaning that gets attached to words and gestures. The photographic director saying, "Shoot him!" means something very different from the gang leader speaking to his crony about you. Likewise, the words we use will be misunderstood, if they are out of sync with the context and with our hearers.

The message we preach never changes, but the way we preach and the words we use must change with the times and the circumstances for greater effectiveness. This means we must take time to get to know our audience, to find the common ground, to understand the point of entry to their hearts, so that we communicate saving truth in terms they understand and can identify with.

Jesus was a master at this. Watch Him as He called the disciples to follow Him. He told them He would make them "fishers of men" (Matt. 4:19). That did it. That kind of language immediately resonated with these Galilean fishermen. Watch Him with farmers, He spoke to them about sowing and reaping, and about weeds and wheat; with the woman at the well, it was about water. With Zaccheus, it was business terms; with Pilate-it was political language. The words and examples that Jesus used were filled with imagery familiar to the people he addressed.

TO BE EFFECTIVE WE MUST FOLLOW HIS EXAMPLE!

Effective evangelism demands that we communicate contextually. In this post-Christian world this means that we will have to find a new vocabulary for the theological words, the evangelical clichés, the religious and 'churchy' Christian jargon we so readily use. Our mission is not to impress those already saved, **BUT TO REACH THE LOST!** It is their ears and hearts we want to reach. Like Paul on Mars Hill, we need to be able to quote some of their literature. Like Peter, on the Day of Pentecost, we must be able to use the context of the moment, like he used the accusation about drunkenness to launch his message about the dynamic of relationship with Jesus Christ through the Spirit of God. In the words of that vintage Youth for Christ slogan, we must be "geared to the times, but anchored to the Rock!"

Ladies and Gentlemen, brothers and sisters, the Biblical strategy we must pursue is creative in approach and contextual in application, as well as **COOPERATIVE IN OPERATION.**

Yes, we must be cooperative in our operation. Jesus taught his disciples to work together. For three years they worked together. After His ascension they worked together in evangelizing Jerusalem, Judea, Samaria and to the ends of the then known world. Jesus knows the strength there is in unity, in working together rather than in isolation. This was the burden of His High Priestly prayer in John chapter 17. A principle demonstrated in the Book of Acts and repeated again and again throughout the epistles. It is the particular ministry of the Holy Spirit to foster this unity and cooperation, and it is our particular sin when we work against spiritual unity.

We must see ourselves as "God's fellow-workers"(1 Cor. 3:9). Not in competition, but in cooperation. As the Scripture says, "The man who plants and the man who waters have one purpose, and each will be rewarded according to his own labor" (1 Cor. 3:8).

The unfinished task demands the concerted, cooperative operations of God's people. The folks in Jerusalem working with folks in Antioch. Paul working with Barnabas and Silas and Timothy and Luke, supported by the gifts of the saints in Macedonia ... and together reaching their world for Christ. We too must be cooperative in our operations.

Fourthly, we must be **COMPELLING IN OUR PRESENTATION**.

The evangelist must be a person with "fire in his belly." We cannot preach soul saving truth in a listless or lackadaisical manner. It takes the intensity of our words and our postures to convey to our audience the urgent importance of what we present. We deal with matters of life and death. Men and women must sense that we are in earnest when we speak of the sinner's plight under the judgment of a holy God, when we declare the good news of man's only reprieve through the death and resurrection of Christ Jesus, and when we issue the summons for them to repent and believe. They must sense that we deeply yearn to see them turn from their lives of sin and estrangement from God and find forgiveness, pardon and salvation through Christ.

This is the compelling message that we must deliver with passion, intensity and soul stirring urgency. Please, please, stay away from evangelistic preaching until your heart is seized with this sense of divine urgency. Stay on your knees until God breaks your hearts over the sinners' awful destiny.

Like John the Baptist of old, be a blazing torch to this generation. No harmless homilies for him. No safe politically correct preaching. No bland boring presentation. NO! He was arresting, exciting, anointed of God, courageous, pointed, penetrating, dynamic ,in a word--compelling! Like Peter on the day of Pentecost. Bold, passionate, pointed, preaching under the power of the Holy Spirit, skillfully using the Scriptures, preaching the Cross, preaching the miracle of resurrection. This kind of preaching touches the hearts of men and women so they cry out under conviction, "What shall we do?" (Acts 2:37).

To become this kind of passionate and persuasive communicator we must spend time with God. To become this kind of compelling communicator we must spend time honing our communications skills, so we can convey God's message with the right Scriptural references,

crafted in words and images suitable to our
audiences, in relevant and compelling style. To
become this kind of passionate, persuasive and
effective communicator **WE NEED THE
ANOINTING OF THE HOLY SPIRIT** ... for
effective impactful preaching is never in the
energy of the flesh. Brothers and sisters, seek the
touch of God, the cleansing and infilling of the
Holy Spirit before you walk to that platform. Let
the message first flow over your soul and do its
work in your spirit before you preach it to
others. Then as you stand you will be a channel,
an instrument yielded to the Spirit of God.
Praise God, we do not stand alone. The Holy
Spirit works in us and with us and through us,
to penetrate the hearts of men and bring
conviction and response to the Gospel
proclaimed. This is His sovereign work ... and
His alone.

One last thing. Evangelistic preaching means
that we must preach for a verdict. Nothing so
puts a cutting edge on our preaching as when
we preach for a verdict, and no verdict is as
compelling as the call to trust Christ for
salvation. Let us not shrink from confronting
people with the claims of Jesus Christ and the
need for deliberate decision. Preach for a
verdict! Preach for a verdict concerning Jesus
Christ and the saving work He accomplished at
the Cross. Let this stamp of evangelism be upon

all you ministry. Sermons without this stamp of evangelism all too often degenerate into good advice rather than the Good News of the Gospel. *We must preach for a verdict*!

TO COMMUNICATE EFFECTIVELY...

- We must be creative in our approach
- We must be contextual in our application
- We must be cooperative in our operation
- We must be compelling in our presentation
- This is the Biblical strategy we must pursue!

My brothers and sisters, if you and I as evangelists are going to communicate effectively in evangelizing this generation...

I. THERE IS A BIBLICAL MESSAGE WE MUST PROCLAIM
II. THERE IS A BIBLICAL INTEGRITY WE MUST POSSESS
1THERE IS A BIBLICAL STRATEGY WE MUST PURSUE...

In other words:
- We must be clear about our Biblical mandate.
- We must be faithful to the Scriptures in our message.

- We must be holy in our personal lives.
- We must be sensitive to our different audiences.
- We must be specific in inviting a decision for Christ.

THE EVANGELIST COMMUNICATES EFFECTIVELY WHEN THE EVANGELIST COMMUNICATES BIBLICALLY!

Let us go back home committed to *"doing the work of an evangelist ... to making full proof of our ministry!"*

Amen!

Appendix 2

Message by Gerry O. Gallimore
delivered at the annual *National Leaders Prayer Breakfast* at the Kingston Pegasus Hotel to Jamaica's top leaders in politics, church, legal field, diplomats, business and trade union leaders --January 1987.

"MY BROTHER'S KEEPER"

Scripture Reading: Genesis 4: 1 – 10

Your Excellency the Most Hon. Sir Florizel Glaspole, the Rt. Hon. Prime Minister and members of the Cabinet; Your Excellences of the Diplomatic Corp; distinguished national leaders; distinguished visitors to our island; ladies and gentlemen; brothers and sisters; fellow Jamaicans, the members of the Organizing Committee have done me a great honor in asking me to address you today. At the same time I am painfully conscious that they have done me a great disservice in expecting that I will be able to follow the distinguished leaders who have occupied this role in previous years.

Once again as a Church we have called you

together for this brief time of spiritual
reflection and upliftment with the hope that
in the light of what God says to us we will make
this a time for sincere resolutions.

Not only will the events of 1986 come into our
minds at this time, but we are conscious that
today is the birthday of that great international
hero, Dr. Martin Luther King, who will be
appropriately remembered in tonight's
celebration. We recognize as well that 1987
marks the 25th anniversary of our nationhood.
25 proud years of managing our own affairs,
charting our own course and determining our
own destiny. As a nation we have not been
without our problems, mistakes, trials and
tribulations, but today I am still proud to be a
Jamaican and proud of the achievements of my
country. We are not nearly where we want to
be, we are not even where we ought to be, but 25
years is a short time — so give us time and with
God's help we expect to march boldly into the
future.

We have a rich heritage as a people and owe a
large debt of gratitude to many noble leaders,
agencies and institutions. 1 say however,
without fear of contradiction, that when an
honest assessment is made of where and to
whom our greatest debt is owed we will find
that we owe more as a nation to Almighty God

than to any other. We must pause now and again and again to thank Him, to honor Him and to trace His great hand of mercy and blessing in our history. God has generously endowed this country with abundant beauty and with many natural resources. As good as these are no one will question that OUR BEST ASSETTS ARE OUR PEOPLE. What a grand mixture! All of us transplanted here by beautiful or ugly circumstances to provide this country with a people of every ethnic background, every shade of skin and every texture of hair imaginable.... to make *"out of many ONE PEOPLE."*

With thoughts of our people in mind I would like to read five verses from that beloved Book which above all others has influenced our lives and from which the theme on our backdrop comes.

READ GENESIS 4:8-12

Here at the very beginning of human history God establishes the principle that we are our brother's keeper. It was a message that was to be reiterated again and again by precept and example in both Old and New Testaments. In the story of Joseph and his 11 brothers; in the story of Jonathan and David; and David and Saul; in the righteous indignation of the prophets against how the rich and powerful

treated the poor and the weak. In the teachings
of Jesus, in His parables culminating in the
Parable of the Good Samaritan. We are our
brother's keeper! This is what God is reminding
us of as a nation this morning.

Ladies and gentlemen, if this is going to mean
anything to us it seems to me that we must first
**AFFIRM THAT HE IS INDEED OUR
BROTHER** and we must understand something
of what it means to be our brother's keeper.

What we have stated positively in our theme
was first posed as a question, *"Am I my
brother's keeper?"* To be our brother's
keeper means:
1. that we are actively involved in seeking
    his welfare and well-being;
2. that we watch protectingly for his life;
3. that we are lovingly concerned about the
    quality of his existence and his
    circumstances;
4. that we care for him as a person and
    accord him the dignity of his personhood.

Now although it was a very long time ago that
this question was posed it is clear that the family
of the Cain-ites are still very much with us. Men
and women who do not wish to acknowledge
their common bond with all humanity, their
fraternal ties to all of God's creation, their

inescapable relationship to their less fortunate brothers. But brothers and sisters, we do belong and are related to each other by the fact that the same Divine Father fashioned us all from the same creative substance, and we all trace our family line back to the same first parents. We further belong to each other by virtue of sharing citizenship of this same country, Jamaica. Whereas the selfish uncaring standards of the world would set us apart from each other saying everyman for himself, God is hereby saying NO, we must not live by such a debased standard that denies fraternity, community and solidarity.

We must affirm our relationship with little brother as well as big brother, with poor brother as well as those better off, with our garbage scrounging brothers and sisters as well as those that manage to feed themselves on more appetizing fare. If this country is to avoid anarchy and move forward with the stability so desperately pleaded for, <u>we must actively became our brother's keeper.</u> We must begin by affirming him, affirming that he exists, and that even in his squalor HE IS OUR BROTHER and he is my neighbor!

SECONDLY, if we are to be our brother's keeper we cannot just hear a **PLEA TO AFFIRM HIM;** we must also have a **PLEDGE TO ASSIST HIM,** to help deliver him from his distress. As we

look around this land we cannot miss that many
of our Jamaican brothers and sisters live in
unacceptable circumstances.

The Scriptures indicate quite clearly that God
loves equally all of humanity and has provided
salvation in His Son on the same terms for all.
But Scripture equally portrays God as having a
special identification with the poor, the hungry,
the naked, the widows and the orphans and
consistently defends their cause. The Scriptures
that we love so much are full of evidence of
God's unashamed bias towards the needy and
the defenseless. If our country is to prosper
and move towards the stability we are pleading
for, then we must follow the Father's example
and actively became our brother's keeper with a
serious commitment to assist him. Proverbs
19:17 says, *"He who is kind to the poor lends to
the Lord."* What a statement! Helping a poor
person is like making a loan to the Lord!

We have just came through Christmas when we
celebrated the Incarnation, God's most complete
statement of His identification with the poor. His
Son Jesus Christ was born to parents too poor to
secure a room in the Inn of Bethlehem, too poor
to offer the normal purification offering of a
lamb; instead they brought two pigeons to the
Temple. Jesus was a humble itinerant preacher
without a salary, never owned a house, couldn't

pay the taxes without help, and was buried in a
borrowed grave. Only as we see Him in the
form of a poor Galilean can we begin to
understand His words, *"1 was hungry and you
gave me food, thirsty and you gave me drink,
naked and you clothed me, in prison and you
visited me."* We must have a pledge to assist
our poor brothers for Jesus says, *"As you do it
to one of the least of these my brethren, you do
it to Me."*

God the Father is asking each one of us today,
"Where is your brother?" Can you see him,
dirty, hungry, naked with no one to care? By
this question the Father wants to establish the
great law that we are responsible for each other's
welfare and in some mysterious and terribly
awesome way, when we minister to their needs
<u>we minister to Him</u>. We dare not 1ook away,
pretend they are not there, put on our social
blinkers and walk by on the other side,
because in so doing we may he missing out on a
opportunity to minister to our blessed Lord.
We must look on the poor and destitute with
new eyes and resolve to heal their hurts and
relieve their misery. We must pledge in fear and
trembling not to kill Him again. Such is the
profound dimension of being our brothers
keepers.

If we truly want this country to prosper, to avoid

anarchy and to move forward in this 25th year of

anarchy and to move forward in this 25th year of
nationhood, then we must: not only hear the
plea to affirm our brothers and heed the need for
a pledge to assist him, but we must also have the
PLUCK TO ACCOST HIM.   Yes, if we are to be
our brother's keeper we must have the pluck to
accost him, the courage to confront him. We
must point out to the brother as well as to the
whole family when we are straying and where
we have gone off track.

The first time these words were used as I read
from the book of Genesis, it was out of a
situation of confrontation. Cain had killed his
brother and God would not let him escape the
tragedy of his action nor the consequences of his
dastardly deed. *"Where is your brother? His
blood cries out to me from the ground."* God the
Lord was confronting the violence, the hate, the
envy, the jealousy, the shedding of blood.

It still grieves God today. The human heart has
not changed and these sins are still rampant in
our land.

Many died by violent death in 1986. Life is still
cheap. The guns are still barking. But it is not
only by the gun that we destroy lives. We do it
by innuendo, by vicious slander and by ugly
lies. We do it by drugs -- be it ganja, alcohol,
cocaine, crack or whatever. Far too many in this

land are peddling this kind of death. We endanger international travel and the transport lifeline of our national economy, but worst of all is the devastation that this heinous trade has on the human personality. We commend the public resolve of government to destroy this evil. We must all say no to this madness; No to this demonic, mind blowing, distressing, slow death. We must unite as a country to oppose this cancerous malady and to root it out regardless, whether it is covered by privilege or profit. If we are to be our brother's keeper, we must have the pluck to accost the corruption in our land. Things move at a snail's pace with endless frustrations that support the conviction of many that very few things happen expeditiously unless a palm is greased.

To be our brother's keeper we must have the guts to confront the issue of the quality of our family life. Too many of our children are growing up without the love and attention of a father, without a Mom and Dad living together in harmony to provide a model worth reproducing. 74% of our children are born out of wedlock. That is a national disgrace in a country where the Church has had such a wide influence. It is time our men buried the 'ram goat mentality' and stop sire-ing children they have no intention of truly fathering. This madness has to stop if we are to truly improve the quality of life for the future.

What we need is a Crusade for Righteousness in this land, for it is *"righteousness that exalts a nation"* but *"sin"* says the Bible *"is a reproach to any people."*   Righteousness is the route to national greatness, is what the Word of God would say to us today. And righteousness implies a serious commitment to justice. My brothers and sisters the expectation of justice is a human right which is built into the fabric of the human spirit by Gcd Himself. Our people must have confidence in our institutions and the poor must have access to the means of redress. Where people lose confidence in our institutions and in the means of obtaining redress they may be tempted to resort to means of their own making.

The call in this 1987 Breakfast is that we be our brother's keeper. The call is for us to consider the well-being of this land and reject violence as a method of settling disputes or effecting social or political change. We must say no to those who incite, provoke or organize violence. No to those who would set one community against another, polarize our society, widen divisions, feed distrust and fuel the fires of disharmony and chaos. We must equally allow freedom to our citizens for peaceful assembly to call public attention to their grievances by those means guaranteed by our Constitution.

If peace is to prevail in our society, we must lay down the weapons of destruction and take up the tools of production. We must lay aside the offensive talk that inflames and engage in the helpful talk that promotes harmony and peace. We have too much to lose in 1987 if we walk any other path.

We understand well the entrenched political traditions of our people and how deeply emotive we feel about our politics. We understand the cut and thrust of party rivalry, the lively debates on national issues, the rising tempo of the contest for national power. We remind our leaders that we are deeply committed to that democracy enshrined in our Constitution and to the legitimate expectations it is designed to preserve for the governed as well to our governors.

We are called to be our brother's keepers which means we must not only affirm him, and assist him, and accost him, but at some point we should pause to **APPLAUD HIM.** I appeal to you my brothers and sisters, whether you be preacher, politician or business-person, don't keep putting down this country every time you speak as if it is the worse place on earth. IT ISN'T!! We must not make such a habit of

<u>trotting out our ills that we forget our blessings</u>.
If we do, then we must not be too surprised
when other people taking the cue from us, write
off this country with nasty epithets. As a nation
we have achieved some things worthy of
commendation and we have produced some
outstanding brothers and sisters of whom we
can be justly proud.

I am proud of the world calibre of leadership we
have produced in the fields of law, in
agriculture, in music, in medicine, in sports, in
the performing arts, in business and in
churchmanship.   Proud of the women of our
land, women like Lady Allan, Lady Bustamante,
Mrs. Edna Manley, Hon. Louise Bennett.   I am
proud of the leadership we have produced in the
field of national politics. I stand tall as a
Jamaican when I think of leaders such as Marcus
Mosiah Garvey. Proud of Sir Alexander
Bustamante, Norman Washington Manley.

Proud of our contemporary leaders such as our
beloved Governor-General, the Most Hon. Sir
Florizel Glaspole, Rt. Hon. Hugh Shearer; Hon
Robert Lightbourne.   I am proud of Mr. Michael
Manley, President of the Peoples National Party
and a distinguished former Prime Minister. Mr.
Michael Manley made the poor among us
visible; he awakened public conscience and
heightened social awareness. The People's

National Party under his leadership has acted with restraint and have not irresponsibly inflamed social tensions.

I am proud of the Rt. Hon. Edward Seaga and the strong leadership he has provided this country during tough times. I am proud of his bold innovative initiatives within this country and within the Caribbean. Despite the unnatural situation of a one-party Parliament, he and his colleagues have governed with restraint.

The reprisals which many feared never occurred, and tensions within the society have been greatly reduced, the poor have had access to funding and training through Solidarity, Self-Start and the HEART Trust programs.

The mercantile community is no longer the domain of a few select families. The base has been spread to include a whole new breed of small people.

We must give credit for the vibrancy in the Tourism sector, for a clean city, for considerable improvement in the delivery of light and power, water and telephone, and for securing the kind of IMF terms you have announced to the nation. While the problems of education remain, we note with relief that there has been a lowering of tensions between government and the teaching profession.

In the Breakfast of last year in this very hall we witnessed as God in His sovereign grace brought our two political leaders together for a solemn moment of prayer. In July when it seemed as if political violence would raise its ugly head once again, they toured the troubled area together and there was peace. And all across this nation that night when it was shown on television, the hearts of our people swelled with pride, a sense of gratitude and admiration rose from the belly-bottom of all of us. We applaud you. Do it again...if necessary!

Let us not forget that our Leaders pay a tremendous price to preside over our affairs...a cost that often takes its toll in their personal lives and health. I want today to pay them a small tribute of appreciation.

I wish also to commend the men and women who by diligence, creativity, hard and honest work, have succeeded against tough odds. We dare not make success appear a crime, or have negative attitudes towards those who enjoy the rewards of their success. We will do these brothers and sisters and our country a disservice if by direct statement or by inference it should appear that we are glorifying poverty, excusing laziness or condemning success. No...that is

not what we are saying at all. We are rather
calling on those who have succeeded to display
a sense of Christian stewardship, and to respond
compassionately to those who have not yet
made the grade, or who may never make the
grade.

We must be careful however, because the virus
of greed is sometimes spawned in the very soil
of success. Our country is proud of its diligent,
honest hard-working successful sons and
daughters, especially those who recognize the
debt they owe to God and to the society in which
they succeeded.

I would be failing if I did not equally applaud
the sterling efforts of our doctors and nurses, our
teachers and policemen, and the many other
diligent workers who give sacrificial service,
often under adverse conditions and with
inadequate remuneration. If we are going to be
our brother's keeper then we should not wait
until his funeral to shower him with encomiums,
let us give him a little applause while he can still
hear it.

And finally, I believe that if we are truly going to
be our brother's keeper we must **AWAKEN
HIM** to his urgent need to seek God, to come to
terms with God's existence, to recognize the
need to get to know God, and then in humility to

surrender our lives to God and to His service. Let me say to you that no matter how well we do in any or every of the other departments about which we have spoken SUCH WILL NOT COMPENSATE FOR FAILURE AT THIS POINT. At the centre of every man's life is the need for God, the need to find spiritual reality. To neglect this important matter is to court disaster in the face of life's unavoidable tests. Hear what the God of Heaven says in His Holy Word, the Bible:

--"*Unless the Lord builds the house, the builders labor in vain*"

   (Ps. 127 1)

-- ''*Seek first the kingdom of God and His righteousness and all*

   these things shall be added unto you" (Matt . 6:33)

-- "*Blessed is the nation whose God is the Lord*" (Ps. 33:12.)

My brothers and sisters, as a nation and as individuals within that nation we have sinned and strayed from God and from His righteousness standards for our lives. We cannot sin and get away with it. We cannot deal unrighteously with our brothers and with the well-being of our land, and get away with it. Behold even now God Almighty is saying to us, *"the voice of your brother's blood cries to me from the ground."* God sees and knows about whom we have killed, whom we have hurt, the lives we have destroyed by our evil practices, how we have bled the poor by the unconscionable prices we have charged, how we have endangered the economy of the nation by the drug trade and how we have failed in the secret places of our personal lives. God knows about our failure and we stand in danger of His judgment unless we repent and turn to Him. I call upon all of us in this our beloved island to make the God of Heaven, Yahweh; the God of the Bible – to make Him THE GOD of this nation so that we may qualify for His blessing and favor and find the strength to love and live for our brothers.

I call upon all of us to realize that we are our brothers' keepers so we must deal righteously, justly and uprightly with him, remembering that *"righteousness exalts a nation but sin is a reproach to any people"* (Prov. 14:34). The standard is high and we are so weak, but do not despair. Our God is a loving and merciful God and He knows us better than we know ourselves. That's why He sent His Son Jesus Christ into the world. By His death on the Cross He has procured for us salvation and the forgiveness of our sins and releases to us the enabling to live righteous lives through the power of the indwelling Holy Spirit when we turn to Him in sincerity and humility.

Like Martin Luther King Jr, I too have a dream, a
dream of a better day for this country as we
affirm that everyman is my brother, sharing a
common human dignity and endowed with
certain fundamental and inalienable human
rights. I dream of a better day when none of our
brothers or sisters have to eat out of garbage
cans <u>because we care enough to assist them</u>. A
better day when corruption, drug trafficking and
injustice are reduced and righteousness prevails.
A better day when more of our people serve the
true and living God, read His Word, go to His
house and order our lives according to His
standards.

If you share this dream at all, then something
must begin here today and hopefully spread like
ripples on a pond till it touches everything and
everyone in this beloved land.

This could be the beginning of a brighter future
if today as leaders <u>we </u>first set right our personal
relationship with God, determining by His grace
to truly make Him our God; to love Him, serve
Him and obey Him. And secondly, to go out
from here with the determination under God, to
set right our relationship <u>with,</u> and our
responsibility <u>to </u>our brothers and sisters.

<u>We are our brother's keeper</u>. Let us therefore in
the bond of humanity **affirm him**, in the light of

Scripture **assist him**, in the pursuit of
righteousness accost **him**, in the name of fair
play **applaud him**, and in the discharge of our
Christian duty **awaken him** to the knowledge
and the saving love of God in Jesus Christ, and
of God's sure and certain judgment on sin and
unrighteousness.

Let us hear the conclusion of this whole matter
as it falls from the lips of Jesus Christ Himself,

**"YOU SHALL LOVE THE LORD YOUR GOD
WITH ALL YOUR HEART, AND WITH ALL
YOUR SOUL, AND WITH ALL YOUR MIND.
THIS IS THE FIRST AND GREAT
COMMANDMENT.**

**AND THE SECOND IS LIKE IT: YOU SHALL
LOVE YOUR NEIGHBOUR AS YOURSELF.**

**ON THESE TWO COMMANDMENTS HANG
ALL LAW AND THE PROPHETS."**
(Matt. 22: 37-40)

AMEN!

Appendix 3: Family & Noteworthy Photos

Lifford G. & Lillian B. Coke

Sonia Gallimore

Gerry Gallimore praying with
former Jamaica Prime Minister Michael Manley
and then current Prime Minister, Rt. Hon.
Edward Seaga at the National Leadership
Prayer Breakfast, Jamaica Pegasus Hotel January
1987

With Jamaica's Prime Minister, P.J. Patterson at
the National Leadership Breakfast at Jamaica
Pegasus Hotel January 1999

Gerry & Sonia with Dr. & Mrs. Werner Burklin

Youth For Christ pics

With YFC Founding President Dr. Torrey
Johnson

161

With renowned Dr. Billy Kim of Korea YFC

With members of the former Jamaica YFC
Chorale

With Dr. & Mrs. Stephen Olford at Amsterdam
2000

Gerry with staff at Mead Johnson (Ja.) Ltd. 1968

164

Son Oliver's baptism

Son Oliver's Ordination

Daughter – Lisa, and her family + Gabby,
Trudy's daughter

A favorite activity. Fishing Trip with my brother
Rupert and my grandchildren

With Rev. Jim Groen, President YFCI at my graduation from Denver Seminary in 1987

1994 – Awarded D.D. By Caribbean Graduate School of Theology. Presented by Dr. Dieumeme Noelistic, Principal of CGST.

Claude Marshall and Las Hutchinson singing at my installation as Pastor of Metropolitan Baptist Church, Miami 1997

Installation of Pastor Arthur Connor as Pastor at Metropolitan Baptist

Daughter – Trudy, and her family